E A

Game Cooking

124 Savory,
Home-tested,
Money-saving
Recipes and Menus
for Game Birds
and Animals

JOAN CONE

50

Easy Game Cooking

124 Savory, Home-tested, Money-saving Recipes and Menus for Game Birds and Animals

JOAN CONE

EPM
PUBLICATIONS

To my husband, Arthur, a jovial hunting companion, and a joy to cook for.

ISBN 0-914440-01-2
Library of Congress Catalog Number 74-75347
© 1974 EPM PUBLICATIONS, INC., MCLEAN, VA.
Distributed by Hawthorn Books

Cover and Book Designed
by Thomas Morley

Table of Contents

A Note From The Author

What, another cookbook? A good question. There's a definite need, though, for this one. Most books dealing with wild game cookery fall into two basic groups. Some are elaborate gourmet texts featuring complicated recipes that use lots of heavy cream and hard-to-find ingredients. The other kind are little more than notes pasted together by outdoorsmen with a fondness for bacon fat — and a limited knowledge of cooking.

You will find this book different. It is designed for the housewife or bachelor (male or female) who wishes to feed the family or provide guests quickly and efficiently with a delectable game dinner. All my recipes and menus are personally tested. I guarantee they will work for you. If you can scramble eggs, you can certainly handle every recipe in this book.

There are some excellent reasons for cooking game. Obviously, with food prices rising game can be used to help you maintain a balanced budget. Hunting, therefore, provides a bonus you don't get through other sports. After all, you cannot eat football tickets or golf balls. In addition, it's fun to add variety to your diet. Game offers a wonderful and tasty change from beef, pork, lamb and chicken. If you have no hunters in your family, friends and neighbors will sometimes give you game. Or you may buy domestic rabbits at supermarkets, and game-farm-raised quail and pheasants at specialty markets. Though not wild, the latter may be prepared with the recipes in this book.

Game is easy to prepare. If it weren't, you and I

1

wouldn't be here. After all, during prehistoric times, game was the *only* meat, and human beings lived primarily by hunting. Our distant ancestors gathered roots, grains and berries whenever they could, but they lived largely on wild game. They had the best of reasons: game was available all year. As we became civilized, cattle, sheep, goats, swine, horses and other animals were domesticated and became available as food. Game consequently became less important to the human diet.

Incidentally, our very first domesticated animal was our faithful friend, the dog. He helped man with his hunting and shared in the rewards.

As civilization progressed and human populations increased, game became less plentiful. By the early Middle Ages, all hunting in Europe was reserved exclusively for the aristocracy. Robin Hood, you may recall, risked execution by poaching deer in Sherwood Forest. The medieval noblemen killed and ate huge amounts of game, but commoners had very little game and not much of anything else for their tables.

Then a new world, America, was discovered. In this land game once again was cheap and abundant for everyone. Here there were no restrictions, no preserves. Wildlife in colonial times was regarded as a nuisance to be slaughtered as rapidly as possible. Later, in the nineteenth century, our transcontinental railroads were built on the buffalo, antelope, elk, and bighorn sheep killed by professional hunters to feed the workmen.

For city folk, market hunters provided prairie chicken, venison, passenger pigeons, railbirds, wild duck, buffalo and other game in abundance. Prices were low. At one time you could buy a 20-pound turkey for fifty cents or an entire deer for a dollar.

By the end of the nineteenth century, market

2

gunning and shrinking habitat for game had the results you might expect. In many areas, game was wiped out. By World War I, it was estimated that the pinelands of New Jersey contained about fifty deer. In other states, game populations were equally low. Kansas and Missouri were among those states in which the deer season, once established, was closed for generations.

It took the leadership of President Theodore Roosevelt and other sportsmen to bring about our modern short hunting seasons, license fees, and enforcement of the game laws by state officers or wardens. Legislation, and the improvement of our environment with the help of sportsmen's dollars, have reversed the decline.

Today game is again available. There is so much game it is estimated that a half-million deer in the United States are killed annually by motorists. In Pennsylvania alone 26,000 deer are killed each year by cars. The abundant game populations are thriving thanks to regulated hunting.

The harvest of this hunt is a valuable source of delicious protein. "Delicious" is, of course, a matter of taste, and our tastes do change. The gamey flavor that many people associate with game birds and animals is the taste people formerly preferred. This taste isn't necessary. We don't have to hold to obsolete tastes any more than we do to outmoded standards of beauty. Who finds the overweight ladies of the Renaissance attractive nowadays?

It should be noted that in England today pheasants and other birds are still hung outdoors uncleaned until they are actually rotting. Only then are they considered properly hung and fit to eat. This peculiar tradition dates all the way back to the time when refrigeration was not available and meat was expected to be spoiled.

3

Oddly enough, spoiled meat doesn't seem to bother the human digestive system. Of course, spoiled fish and eggs are another matter.

In this country we have virtually eliminated most of that old gamey flavor by the way we care for game in the field and by the way we cook it. You will notice that all the recipes in this book are simple enough so that the interesting special taste of game comes through. It seems to me almost sinful to drown a pheasant in so much cream sauce it tastes exactly like chicken, or prepare delicious venison to make it indistinguishable from veal or beef. My aim is to make your game meals both tasty and enjoyable, and provide you with a welcome change from everyday fare.

Wine is used in many of these recipes to keep the game moist and to enhance the flavor. If you prefer, substitute chicken broth or apple cider for white wine and beef broth for the red wine.

Sanitation, refrigeration and modern kitchens allow us to have meat from the store with no spoilage. We should insist that meat from forest or field be fresh and properly cared-for too. Game birds, waterfowl and small animals aren't much trouble. They should be gutted and washed out as soon as possible and then chilled. Big game can be more difficult to handle. The same rules, however, apply: Kill it quickly, clean it at once, cool it as rapidly as possible.

You will continue to find people who insist that all game, especially big game, must be hung. Don't believe them. Freezing accomplishes all that hanging ever did and without risk of tainting your meat. Freeze game and forget it until it is time to consider cooking it. This way, if you'll pardon the pun, you'll find yourself ahead of the game. Because water expands when it freezes, freezing game breaks down the cellular

4

structure of the meat, making it much more tender. Hanging does the same thing, but through decomposition.

One objection to all game comes from women who naturally dislike being faced in their kitchen by a rabbit, pheasant, or goose in the appealing state nature made it except for being very dead. They have a valid point.

Our mothers or grandmothers thought nothing of taking an axe, killing a chicken, cleaning it, plucking it, cutting it up, and cooking it. Today, we no longer *have* to do it, and many of us absolutely refuse.

It seems logical to me that the hunter is responsible for delivering game to his wife in the state she is prepared to cope with. Certainly, the hunter should clean the game. He shot it, didn't he? Therefore, it's up to him to finish the job. As for plucking and skinning, every waterfowl and most pheasant areas have local residents who will handle this task for a small fee. Otherwise, let the mighty hunter do it, or at least assist you. With deer and other big game, it's a good idea to use a neighborhood butcher. A phone call to a cold storage plant (or locker rentals) will put you on to one who will handle your deer, elk, moose or whatever at a minimal charge. He might want to keep the hide as part payment.

If you are a lady hunter, huntress, hunter person, or whatever, you'd better buy a pair of rubber gloves and leave your squeamishness behind. Actually, there's nothing to cleaning most animals. I find fish, with their scales and odor, considerably worse to handle.

I've given easy instructions for cleaning, plucking or skinning game animals and birds in the appropriate sections. Under Big Game, Small Game, Upland

Game Birds and Waterfowl you'll find the general directions before the recipes.

To help you plan complete dinners around your favorite game I've included menus at the end of each section. Under Accompaniments are the recipes for the vegetables, salads, starches, hot breads and desserts in each menu.

Microwave ovens are the latest in cooking. Because these ovens cook so quickly, they are excellent for preparing small quantities. I've included recipes for venison, dove and quail at the close of the book.

We've come a long way from medieval hanging to microwave ovens. Game animals and birds are now not only much easier to prepare, but they have never tasted better. I know because I have personally prepared and eaten each of the recipes and meals that follow. Here's wishing you and your family the same pleasure they have brought me and mine.

BIG GAME

In Virginia the wild turkey is considered a big game animal. Arizona lists the javelina or peccary. Most of us, however, when we think of big game refer to the deer family.

Whitetail and mule deer provide America's larders with an estimated one hundred million pounds of venison annually. Though elk and moose are less available, they are prepared in virtually identical fashion and according to the same recipes. These recipes will also succeed with caribou, so use them if you live in Alaska. In fact, every North American big game species, with the exception of the bear family, may be prepared exactly as venison. This means that if you can turn out good venison, you are an automatic expert on bighorn sheep, antelope, Dall sheep and so forth.

Sometimes the U.S. Department of the Interior makes buffalo meat available from surplus animals. This meat may be cooked exactly like beef. As for the bear family, young black bear (in any color phase) are considered worth eating. I've never tried any and in this book, I intend to stay with tested recipes and animals and birds I know something about.

How do I know about them?

My husband laughingly claims I'm the only girl who ever became a big game hunter because she went fishing.

During our early years as young marrieds, we took our summer vacations at an Ontario fishing camp. It was a miserable place in an advanced state of dilapidation. Nobody minded because the fishing was wonderful. (I have old home movies to prove it.)

Aside from the fishing, all was bad, and the meals were worst of all. The meat was sinewy and looked and tasted like boiled rubber. I wondered how the owner and his family survived on it all year and nosing into the situation, I found they never tasted it. Instead of eating the horrible beef served paying guests, they dined grandly on moose.

One lantern-lit evening sitting around the smoke-filled kitchen and exchanging fish stories with the owner, several guides, and some other guests, I asked if I might have a taste of moose meat. Actually, I was only curious. For all I knew, it could have been as awful as the beef.

You might have thought my innocent remark was a heinous crime. The noisy kitchen instantly became silent. The camp owner looked at me with narrowed, nasty eyes. His "No" was expressed with vigor. Obviously, he considered moose meat far too good for any of it to be wasted on American vacationers who provided his livelihood.

After a few moments, peace was restored. But, later that night, unable to sleep on my broken-spring cot, I asked my husband to please take me on a moose hunt. "After all," I pointed out, "If it's that good, why don't we have some too?"

He laughed all the way to the bank where he withdrew the money so we could fly up to Newfoundland the following autumn. There each of us succeeded in bagging a moose. I then carefully arranged to have our animals butchered at the leading meat market in Gander, and the meat boned, frozen, and shipped home. Our only problem was at U.S. Customs where the nice gentlemen didn't want to believe a young lady who insisted she was shipping home *two* moose!

Newfoundland moose are not as large as the Alaskan variety. Even so, each amounts to nearly a half-ton of meat on the hoof. With a pair of them in a giant freezer, it was like having a multi-hundred pound boneless ham. In spite of four hungry children and much entertaining we bought no other beef for better than a year.

Moose meat definitely is very good. My children complained bitterly when we returned to eating beef, pork and lamb. Our friends complained too. "Go back and shoot a couple more," they urged. We hope to do exactly that someday. It's a unique experience. A moose hunt is a journey into yesteryear. You live the same way as your ancestors did in a place without roads or towns. You're amid endless woods, wonderful scenery and zero population problems. After boating on crowded Chesapeake Bay, it comes as a shock to reach the shore of a tremendous northern lake and discover....nothing....not a boat, not a house, not even a beer can. I recommend the experience.

Yet, regardless of where you hunt, or even if you never take a rifle down from the wall and saunter outdoors, deer, elk and moose are delicious. The only point to remember is that your animal must be cleaned out immediately, cooled down rapidly and kept cool during the journey home to prevent spoilage of the meat.

States which insist a deer must remain whole while being transported have valid reasons. The objective is to stop you from killing and quartering more than you are entitled to shoot. From the standpoint of the venison itself this is a mistake. Wherever possible, any big game animal should be quartered, even skinned, immediately, then packed in ice for transport.

Of course, with moose and elk you will almost always

have a guide or outfitter to assist you and a minimum of problems. An established outfitter takes pride in caring for your meat.

If you're deer hunting and have no guide, which is very probable, a good reference source is a small book, *The Complete Deer Hunt*, written by Joe DeFalco. It is available from its author at 197 Madison Street, Franklin Square, New York 11010. Mr. DeFalco's hunting advice may not apply to your area, but he claims to have butchered personally more than 5,000 deer for friends and customers, and I believe him. He explains and illustrates exactly how to handle venison from field to freezer in terms everyone can understand and use.

Here are some other points to consider with respect to big game:

1. *Don't grind venison into deerburger before shipping.*

A big game animal is never entirely steaks, roasts and chops. A good portion of it must be ground into chopped meat and used as mooseburger, elkburger or whatever. However, meat once ground tends to spoil very rapidly. My suggestion is to keep aside all chunks of meat you expect to use for grinding, wrap them separately and label "For Ground Meat." Properly wrapped, they may be stored in your freezer or locker plant for as long as you wish.

When you anticipate using ground meat, take a chunk from the freezer and run it over to your butcher before it is completely defrosted. Remind him to add 15-25% beef fat to it while grinding. Any professional butcher will know exactly how much to add. Why add fat in these days of cholesterol? Good question. The answer is that wild animals are not fed as well as domestic stock. They have so little fat that unless a quantity is added your deerburgers will be woefully dry and difficult to cook.

This brings up another point: Because game is so free of fat, and these recipes use so very little, someone with a cholesterol problem may be able to eat game when he is not allowed beef. Check with your doctor, of course.

At home mold your ground meat into patties or wrap in 1 or 2-pound packages. You can figure a pound of ground venison, including added fat, makes four very generous venisonburgers with minimum shrinkage. Then freeze again until ready to use. You may find that refreezing after grinding tends to darken the meat slightly. However, it does not affect taste or flavor and will not cause your meat to spoil.

2. *Wrap steaks, chops and roasts in meal-size portions and mark plainly.*

Would you believe there actually are people who don't know what's in their home freezer? Personally, I like to know what I'm unwrapping. I also want each of my packages to represent an average meal for my family.

Wrap big game in heavy duty aluminum foil or with double strength freezer paper. If you use freezer paper, make a double drugstore fold down the middle to keep out all air. (See diagram.) Tuck in the sides. Then use freezer tape to secure both ends and the middle of the package. With a water-proof marker write on it the type of cut, weight and date. By dating your packages you'll know what to use first.

When you store game in your freezer, place all your steaks in one location, all roasts in another, all ground meat in a third. This makes them easy to locate.

11

DRUGSTORE FOLD

Place food in center of an oblong piece of heavy duty foil large enough to go around food and allow for folding at top and sides. Pad protruding bones with small crumpled pieces of foil.

Bring two sides up and over the food item, match the long ends and fold over about ½ inch. Make a crease the entire length.

Make one more tight fold to bring wrapping down to level of food surface. Press out air towards end to eliminate freezer burns.

Then, molding foil to contours of food item, fold short ends up and over again, continuing to press out air before sealing ends.

If you use heavy duty aluminum foil, be sure to make the double center fold and also fold the ends over several times. You MUST keep all air from your meat or you will have freezer burn, the discoloration that means loss of flavor and texture. How can one write on aluminum foil? One method is to stick on a home-made label of freezer tape and write on that. Or you can find special markers designed to write on aluminum foil.

Now that you've done these things, I hope you're not too exhausted to cook your venison. Please remember all cooking times must be approximate because each game animal, unlike domestic cattle, will vary by age and type of feed consumed in the wild.

Venison [Elk, Moose]

VENISON STEAKS AND CHOPS BROILED OR GRILLED

You'll really appreciate venison steaks and chops, especially from young animals, when you broil or grill them in your oven or on your outdoor grill. Cook the same as similar beef cuts except DO NOT OVERCOOK. Because venison has much less moisture and fat content than beef, it becomes very dry and tough with long broiling or cooking. Best idea is medium rare and then salt or pepper to taste.

VENISON MEATLOAF

Assuming fat has been added to the meat by your butcher or yourself, you can use any standard cookbook recipe for meatloaf. Here is one you may prefer instead. My family and friends find it very good.

1½ pounds ground venison	1½ teaspoons salt
¾ cup uncooked oatmeal	¼ teaspoon pepper
¼ cup onion, chopped	1 cup tomato juice
	1 egg, beaten

Preheat your oven to 350° F. Combine all ingredients. Pack firmly into an ungreased 8½-x4½-x2½-inch loaf pan. Bake for about 1 hour and 15 minutes. Let stand 5 minutes before slicing.
[*Serves 4 to 8*]

CHINESE STYLE VENISON RIBS

Michigan is one of our biggest deer hunting states. Would you believe that more than one million hunting licenses are issued there each year? It's true! This recipe comes from the Upper Peninsula which offers superb deer hunting , and the camp cooks make a specialty of these venison ribs.

4 pounds venison ribs	½ cup water
½ cup soy sauce, Japanese style	4 tablespoons brown sugar
½ cup sherry	2 cloves garlic, crushed

Preheat oven to 350° F. Arrange ribs in a large roasting

pan. Combine all ingredients, stir well, and pour over ribs. Cover pan. Bake 45 minutes turning ribs once or twice. Remove cover and continue cooking until golden brown and thoroughly done. Baste with sauce each time you turn ribs. For crispy ribs be sure to arrange them in a single layer within your roaster.

[*Serves 4*]

VENISON ROAST BAKED IN FOIL

This is delicious, and by using foil you make cleaning up much easier.

3-4 pounds roast	½ envelope dry onion soup

Preheat oven to 425° F. Place roast on an adequate piece of heavy duty aluminum foil. Sprinkle a half envelope of dry onion soup over the meat. Bring edges of foil together and seal tightly. Place in shallow roasting pan and bake for 2 to 2½ hours. You will find ample juice collects within the aluminum foil, and this may be thickened for gravy.

[*Serves 6*]

VENISON, MOOSE OR ELK ROAST IN BAG

My experience with oven cooking bags has been exceptionally good. They do a wonderful job of keeping the juices in the meat and keeping your oven clean too.

2 tablespoons flour
1 cup dry red wine
3-4 pounds venison
  roast
Salt

1 bay leaf
8 whole cloves
1 medium onion, diced
1 teaspoon thyme

Preheat oven to 325° F. Place flour in small (10 x 16-inch) Brown-In-Bag and shake until bag is well coated. Place bag in two-inch deep roasting pan. Pour wine into bag and stir until well mixed with flour. Rub roast with salt. Put meat into bag. Add bay leaf, cloves, onion and thyme around meat. Close bag with twist-tie, and if you are using a meat thermometer, insert thermometer through bag into center of meat. Finally, make 6 ½-inch slits in top of bag near the twist-tie. Cook for 2 hours, or until internal temperature reaches 180° F., or meat is tender. The liquid in the bag is ready to use as gravy or you may thicken it with flour if you prefer.

[*Serves 6 to 8*]

Venison, a lean meat, roasts especially well in an oven bag. The bag keeps in juices and provides rich gravy makings.

GAME STROGANOFF IN PRESSURE COOKER

Pressure cookers are here to stay. They save time and trouble and do a beautiful job of cooking game. This recipe may appear to be complicated since it has a number of ingredients. However, it really is easy to prepare, and the result is superb.

1 ½ pounds venison (or
   other big game) in
   ¾ -inch cubes
Flour, salt and pepper
2 tablespoons shortening

½ cup onion, chopped
1 clove garlic, minced
1 6-ounce can mushrooms
   (reserve liquid)
1 can condensed tomato
   soup
1 tablespoon
   Worcestershire sauce
6 to 8 drops Tabasco sauce
½ teaspoon salt
1/8 teaspoon pepper
1 cup sour cream

Dredge meat in seasoned flour. Heat pressure cooker; melt shortening and brown meat well. Remove cooker from heat. Add onions, garlic, mushrooms and liquid, tomato soup, Worcestershire, Tabasco, salt and pepper. Mix well. Close cover securely, place pressure at 15 pounds and cook 15 to 20 minutes. Cool cooker at once. Add sour cream and simmer (do not boil) for 10 minutes in uncovered cooker. Serve over wide noodles. Sprinkle with Parmesan cheese.
[*Serves 4 to 6*]

GAME STROGANOFF IN SKILLET

If you don't own a pressure cooker and want an easy
way to make venison stroganoff, here's one that is
practically effortless.

½ cup vegetable oil
2 pounds boned venison
   in 1-inch cubes
¼ cup flour

1 envelope onion soup
   mix
3 cups water
1 can condensed cream of
   mushroom soup
6 tablespoons catsup

Begin by heating vegetable oil in a heavy skillet while
shaking meat in flour to coat. Then sauté venison cubes
until browned. Add soup mix and water. Simmer
covered an hour or more until venison is tender. Finally
add cream of mushroom soup and catsup, heat
thoroughly, and serve over noodles or rice.
[*Serves 4 to 6*]

VENISON IN BAG

This is the favorite recipe of Kathy McCormick, a superlative cook who lives with her husband Frank on Maryland's Eastern Shore. That area is overloaded with fish and game, and Frank and Kathy have geese, ducks, rabbits, quail, squirrel, oysters, doves and maybe venison too — all without leaving their own property.

Now, if you wonder why such an experienced cook as Mrs. McCormick would use an oven cooking bag to prepare venison, the answer is that these bags take care of basting and oven cleaning. In the bag meat is basted automatically with its own juices and the added liquid. Thus, your venison will stay moist and cook to a delicious tenderness. There's even an added bonus: little or no cleanup! Also, the bag retains all the juice for a perfect gravy, which you may thicken if you desire.

¼ cup flour
1 cup dry red wine
1 cup water
3-4 pounds roast 4 inches thick
Salt and pepper

2 tablespoons dried basil
1 large onion, chopped
2 bay leaves
2 cloves garlic, chopped
3 large ripe tomatoes, chopped (or a 1-pound can tomatoes)

Preheat oven to 350° F. Place ¼ cup flour in small (10 x 16-inch) oven cooking bag and put bag into a 2-inch deep roasting pan. Fold bag back for easier handling. Slowly add wine and water mixing well with flour. Cover roast with salt and pepper and place in bag with remaining ingredients. Close bag with twist-tie and make 6 ½-inch slits in top of bag. Cook for 2 hours or until tender. (Time will vary with size of cut and age of your deer.)
[*Serves 6 to 8*]

MOOSE OR VENISON BURGUNDY

The first time I ate this delicious dish was after a bitterly cold day afield at Troy, Virginia, and our party returned to the gracious home of Bob and Ginny Gooch. Their 18th century house has been in Bob's family for many generations. Bob is a well-known and much-respected outdoor writer, and Ginny cooks as well as Bob writes.

4 tablespoons margarine
2 pounds moose, elk or venison cut in 1-inch cubes
1 teaspoon salt
3 medium onions, thinly sliced
1 clove garlic, crushed
½ teaspoon dried basil
Grated peel of half a lemon
1 teaspoon paprika

1½ tablespoons flour
1 cup dry red wine
1 cup canned beef broth
½ pound raw mushrooms, chopped or 1 4-ounce can mushrooms
Parsley, chopped

Melt margarine in large Dutch oven and brown meat lightly. Add salt, onions, garlic, basil, lemon peel and paprika. Cover and simmer for 30 minutes. Sprinkle flour over meat and mix well. Add wine and beef stock, cover and simmer for 1 hour. Mix in mushrooms, cover, and simmer until venison is tender — 15 minutes or longer. Then sprinkle with chopped parsley.
[*Serves 4 to 6*]

Here are three recipes sent me by Pat Auld in Texas. She and her husband Dan have many deer on their ranch holdings and serve venison regularly.

VENISON MEAT BALLS TEXAS STYLE

3 slices soft white bread
1 ½ pounds ground
   venison
2 teaspoons salt
1/8 teaspoon oregano
1/8 teaspoon basil
¼ teaspoon pepper
⅔ cup onion, finely
   chopped

¼ cup butter
1 tablespoon flour
1 cup milk
Salt and pepper for gravy

Break bread into small bits and combine with ground venison, salt, oregano, basil, pepper and chopped onion. Blend thoroughly. Shape meat mixture into small balls about 1 inch in diameter. Chill for 15 to 20 minutes. Brown in skillet with butter, turning frequently for even cooking.

Cover pan, reduce heat to low, and cook 15 minutes more. Remove meat balls to a separate pan. Then add flour to drippings in skillet and blend with butter. Add milk until you get the consistency of gravy. Salt and pepper to taste. Return the meatballs to gravy and simmer for another 5 minutes.

[*Serves 6*]

NEW SOUTH VENISON STEAK

¼ cup flour
¾ tablespoon salt
1 dash Cayenne pepper
Pinch of thyme, ground nutmeg and ground cloves
3 pounds venison rump steak
2 tablespoons melted beef suet
3 large onions thinly sliced

2 cups fresh tomatoes, peeled and quartered, or 2 cups stewed tomatoes
1 ½ tablespoons Worcestershire sauce
4 drops Tabasco
1 ½ cups dry red wine
1 clove
½ small clove garlic
2 parsley sprigs
¼ teaspoon dried thyme
1 bay leaf
1 cup sautéed mushroom caps
Salt and pepper

Sift flour with salt, Cayenne, thyme, nutmeg and cloves. Vigorously pound this seasoned flour into venison steak. Cut steak into 1-inch cubes. Melt beef suet in a heavy stewpot or Dutch oven and sear venison on all sides. Add thinly sliced onions. When meat and onions are well browned, add tomatoes, Worcestershire sauce, Tabasco, wine, garlic clove, parsley, thyme and bay leaf. Cover pot tightly. Set in 350° F. oven and cook 2½ hours or until meat is tender. Remove pot from oven and bring to boil over direct heat. Salt and pepper to taste and stir in sautéed mushroom caps. (Pat Auld suggests serving red currant jelly with this.)
[*Serves 8 to 10*]

VENISON NIBBLES

Cut strips of venison steak into pieces 3 inches long and
1 inch wide. Salt and pepper to taste and dip in beaten
egg and then in cracker crumbs. Fry in very hot, deep
grease just like French-fries until golden-brown.
Nibbles can be used for cocktail hors d'oeuvres or an
evening snack for the family.

OVEN VENISON MARINADE

1 tablespoon flour	1 whole clove
2 pounds boneless venison cut into 1-inch cubes	1 clove garlic, minced
1 teaspoon salt	1 stalk celery, sliced
¼ teaspoon thyme	1 cup frozen pearl onions or coarsely chopped onions
4 peppercorns	½ cup dry red wine

Shake 1 tablespoon flour in a small (10 x 16-inch) oven
cooking bag and place in 2-inch deep roasting pan.
Fold bag back for easy handling. Add meat and other
ingredients into bag. Close bag with twist tie and turn
gently to mix contents. Refrigerate several hours,
turning bag occasionally for additional mixing. Preheat
oven to 325°F., remove pan from refrigerator, and
make 6 ½-inch slits in top of bag. Cook for 2 or 2½
hours until tender.
[*Serves 6 to 8*]

DEERBURGER SOUP

This is a very old recipe which comes from the Paul Bunyan country in the upper Middle West. After you try it, you'll agree the "good old days" must have been simply grand.

1-2 pounds deerburger (with added fat)
1 cup onion, diced
1 cup raw potatoes, cubed
1 cup carrots, sliced
1 cup cabbage, shredded
¼ cup rice

Beef concentrate to taste
1 small bay leaf, crushed
½ teaspoon thyme
2 teaspoons salt
1/8 teaspoon pepper
1½ quarts water
1 No. 2 can tomatoes

Brown deerburger and onion in large pot. Add potatoes, carrots and cabbage. Bring to a boil and sprinkle the rice into the mixture. Add all remaining ingredients except for tomatoes. Cover and simmer for 1 hour. Just before serving add tomatoes and skim off any fat.

[*Serves 8*]

VENISON OR MOOSE CASSEROLE

This is an easy recipe to use sometime when you're in a hurry and haven't much time to put a meal on the table. I understand it's based on a recipe which originated in Maine back in the days of moose and caribou in that state. Incidentally, moose are coming back to the point where someday there may be an open season on them again.

2 pounds venison or
    moose meat cubed
1 10¾-ounce can
    mushroom soup

1 envelope dry onion
    soup mix
1 cup canned tomatoes
    or 2 fresh tomatoes

Preheat oven to 325° F. Place meat in a casserole and add mushroom soup, dry onion mix and tomatoes. Cover casserole and bake for 2 hours.
[*Serves 4 to 6*]

DEER/MOOSE OR ELK LIVER

The liver of these big game animals is delicious and should be eaten as soon as possible for the best taste. If you cannot use the liver within 2 or 3 days, freeze it. After it is thoroughly frozen, take the liver to your butcher and have it cut in ½-inch slices. Wrap and place frozen slices in your freezer. When wrapping slices for freezing, place a piece of aluminum foil or freezer paper between each slice to keep them separated. Otherwise, they will freeze together. To cook first allow slices to thaw. Fry two slices of bacon per person in a heavy iron or Teflon-lined skillet. Save sufficient bacon fat to fry liver. Roll liver slices in flour, season with salt and pepper and fry quickly in hot skillet. About five minutes on a side should be adequate. Liver should be pale pink on the inside. Be sure not to overcook because then delicious liver will become dry and tough.

VENISON CHILI

Pat Auld, friend, sportswoman, fellow member of WINRA, and internationally known hunter of big game, gave me this recipe which she uses when entertaining at her sumptuous home in Kerrville, Texas.

3 pounds ground shoulder of venison	1 8-ounce can tomato sauce
	½ teaspoon oregano
1 large onion, chopped fine	2 tablespoons chili powder (adjust to suit your taste)
2 small buttons garlic	Salt and pepper to taste
2 tablespoons fat	Corn meal to thicken

Fry meat, onion, and garlic in fat until meat turns color. Add tomato sauce and seasonings. Simmer 30 minutes. Slowly sprinkle in enough corn meal to thicken until it suits your taste. Add some water if needed. Cook 15 to 20 minutes longer. Serve with kidney beans and rice. This chili may be frozen for future use.

[*Serves 8 to 10*]

QUICK CHILI WITH VENISONBURGER

Here's a recipe with a slight touch of Texas, or Mexico, if you prefer.

1 pound ground venison, moose or elk
¼ cup chopped onion, or 1 tablespoon dry minced onion
1 10-ounce can tomato soup
1 3-pound can kidney beans
1 to 3 teaspoons chili powder

Brown venisonburger and onion in large skillet. (I assume you have added fat to meat when it was ground.) Add tomato soup, kidney beans, including liquid, and chili powder. Then simmer for 15 to 20 minutes. This is excellent served over rice.
[*Serves 4 to 6*]

VENISON SUKIYAKI OR TERIYAKI DINNER

You can easily prepare this delicious meal from the dry packaged dinners found on your supermarket shelves. Or you may prefer to use an Oriental cookbook and make your own sukiyaki or teriyaki using venison in place of beef. Either way and for either dish, you need 1 pound of venison sirloin or round steak sliced into very thin strips. The strips should be approximately ¼ inch thick, ½ inch wide, and 2 to 3 inches long. (It is easiest to cut these strips when the meat is partially frozen.) Brown your venison strips in 2 tablespoons of cooking oil in a large skillet. Finally, follow the directions that come with the prepared dinners or in your Oriental cookbook. Serve on rice.

[*One pound of venison serves 4*]

VENISON SWISS STEAK

This recipe was given to me by Rose Spanel, a lovely young bride married to a wildlife manager with the U.S. Department of Defense. Rose is originally from Wisconsin and learned how to cook venison at home. As a wildlife manager, her husband has a reliable supply of venison. This is one of the advantages of living in a rural area.

1 round steak of venison	Onions, mushroom soup,
Flour, salt, pepper	celery soup, or
	tomatoes are optional

Thoroughly pound your round steak. Then flour, salt and pepper the steak and brown it with shortening in a heavy skillet. Add sufficient water to cover. At this point you may vary the recipe to suit your personal taste by adding onions, mushroom soup, celery soup, or tomatoes. Cover and simmer 1½ hours or until tender. You may need to add water occasionally. (If you use an electric skillet with this recipe, set it at 350° F.)

[*Serves 4*]

MICHIGAN VENISON STEW

Back in the days when Paul Bunyan and his blue ox
were figuring in logging camp folklore, venison was a
basic staple of the lumberers, and boys and girls from
backwoods farms took venison sandwiches to school in
their lunchpails. Stew, handy and simmering over a
wood stove, was a staple relished by all.

1 ½ pounds venison (any
part cut into stew-size
pieces)
6 medium potatoes, cut
into chunks
6 carrots, cut into
chunks
3 celery stalks, cut into
2-inch lengths

1 envelope dry onion
soup
1 8-ounce can tomato
sauce
1 2-ounce can sliced
mushrooms

Preheat oven to 350° F. Place venison, potatoes,
carrots and celery into casserole dish and sprinkle with
onion soup mix. Add tomato sauce and mushrooms.
Cover tightly with lid or aluminum foil and bake 1 ½
hours.
[*Serves 4 to 6*]

VENISONBURGERS

If you grind your own meat, be sure to add beef fat.
Most butchers recommend 25% additional fat. Thus
for each 4 pounds of venison, you would add 1 pound
of beef suet. After molding into patties, sauté, broil or
grill exactly as you would any ordinary hamburger.

VENISON [Moose, Elk, Deer] STEAKS AND CHOPS SAUTÉED

To sauté chops or steaks first melt ½ stick (¼ cup) of butter in a heavy skillet. Add your meat to the hot skillet and turn it often so it will brown nicely on both sides. Then salt and pepper to taste. These cuts of venison are best cooked until the meat is a light pink. (You can check by making a small slit with a sharp knife.) Overcooking makes venison tough. This is why medium rare venison steaks are generally preferred.

VENISON MINCEMEAT

There are few aromas more tantalizing than that of mincemeat cooking. It makes me hungry just to think about it. You can use this mincemeat to make the cake you'll find in the Accompaniments section.

2 pounds cooked venison (chopped in grinder or blender)
4 pounds apple, peeled, cored and chopped
2 pounds raisins
4 cups sugar, brown or white
¾ pound melted suet or butter
½ teaspoon cloves
1 teaspoon mace
½ teaspoon nutmeg
2 teaspoons salt
1 ½ teaspoons cinnamon
Apple cider

After mixing all ingredients add sufficient cider to cover. Cook slowly until all fruits are tender (about 1 hour). This recipe will make 3 to 4 quarts of mincemeat which may be frozen until you are ready to use it.

Big Game Dinner Menu No. 1

VENISON, ELK, MOOSE OR OTHER BIG GAME

　[Prepared as you prefer]

SOUTHERN SPOON BREAD

SWEET AND SOUR RED CABBAGE

ORANGE GLAZED CARROTS

MINCEMEAT CAKE WITH HARD SAUCE

COFFEE

WINE, A DRY RED

Recipes for all accompaniments appear in a special section near the end of the book.

Big Game Dinner Menu No. 2

VENISON, ELK, MOOSE OR OTHER BIG GAME

   [Prepared in any manner]

VEGETABLE YAM CASSEROLE

WALDORF SALAD

PINEAPPLE MERINGUE PIE

COFFEE

WINE, ROSÉ OR ANY DRY RED WINE

All recipes appear in the Accompaniments section.

SMALL GAME

The amount of small game that is shot and cooked each
year in the United States is difficult even to estimate. In
the aggregate it runs into thousands of tons.

Although most of these small game recipes deal
with rabbit and squirrel, I have included one each for
woodchuck, muskrat, raccoon and beaver. These four
animals are all delicious, and too often are shot as pests
or trapped, skinned and the carcasses discarded. In
these days of world-wide protein shortage there is no
sensible reason for wasting good meat out of
squeamishness. If you live in the country and have
neighbors who trap or run coonhounds at night, you
may find that a friendly word to them will bring you
some very fine eating. Frankly, I've never done any
trapping, and some animals used in these recipes were
obtained from Michael D. Spanel, Wildlife Manager
for Camp A.P. Hill in Caroline County, Virginia. These
animals were trapped for the Post Museum where the
hides may be seen mounted in a first-rate habitat
exhibit.

Getting down to the heart of the matter, there's one
tool you'll find essential for all small game, game birds
and waterfowl. It's known as a Wiss kitchen shears, and
bears about as much resemblance to an everyday
poultry shears as a Rolls-Royce does to a Volkswagen.
There's even a safety factor. The kitchen shears, because
of the scissors-like handles, insure your fingers against
slipping.

Both rabbits and squirrels should be cleaned afield.
If it's possible to save the livers and hearts, so much the
better. They are delicious. Skinning the carcasses is
relatively easy, and by using the shears mentioned,
quartering becomes a cinch.

When skinning rabbits, you should *always* wear rubber gloves. Many people don't bother, but tularemia (rabbit fever) is no joking matter. It is a nasty, often fatal illness, caught only by people who skin diseased rabbits bare-handed. The germs enter any little cut in the skin and take off from there. Now that I've scared you half to death, let me say that your chances of contacting tularemia, even without gloves, are virtually zero. But why take chances? Wear rubber gloves and stop worrying. Once skinned, even a sick rabbit is perfectly safe to eat as cooking destroys the bacteria which cause tularemia.

A simple way to skin a rabbit or squirrel is to cut through the skin at the nape of the neck, holding the head in your left hand. Pull the skin off with your right hand. It's attached very loosely and peels right off. Incidentally, you can sell squirrel tails for 25¢ each to the Sheldon Corporation, P.O. Box 508, Antigo, Wisconsin, 54409. Write them for details of this offer. They use the tails in making the Mepps spinners for anglers. Evidently, they always need more tails than are available to them locally.

After skinning, here's what you do next with your small game animals:

1. Clean out all blood and blood clots under running water.
2. Cut rabbits into quarters, and squirrels into halves or quarters.
3. Dry the pieces by draining them on a paper towel before freezing.
4. Wrap in heavy duty freezer paper or with heavy aluminum foil for freezing as with big game.
5. If you prefer, you may freeze the game in plastic freezing bags, but always use two bags, one inside the other, for double strength. Otherwise, jagged

ends of bone can puncture the bag, let air in, and
cause freezer burn.

6. Mark all packages of frozen game as to contents
and date placed in freezer. Then you know what
you've got, and can use the oldest first.

Rabbit

I well remember the problem we had convincing our
small children that Mommy and Daddy had not shot
the Easter Bunny when we came home with our bag of
cottontails. Their woeful cries, however, became
delighted screams for "more, more," when rabbit was
served for dinner. It's good, no question about that.
After eating rabbit several times, the children readily
accepted our promise that we would never shoot any
large white rabbit who lived in a little house in a hole
filled with candy. We've kept that promise too. After
all, I don't want to be known as the lady who cooked
Peter Rabbit!

Rabbits have been around for an extremely long
while. They have outlasted such animals as the
mammoth, the saber-tooth tiger, and wolves the size of
a small grizzly bear. How did they do it against all the
odds, including the added handicap of tasting simply
delicious? There's an answer, of course, but that has
nothing to do with a cookbook.

What is important here is that rabbits, and squirrels
too, are America's most sought-after game. For every
deer-hunter and every sportsman who goes afield with
dog and gun for quail and partridge, there are probably
twenty farm boys, rural store owners, and even
ministers, who go afield primarily for rabbits, generally
with the expert help of one or more beagles.

RABBIT WITH DARK RAISIN GRAVY

This is my husband's favorite game recipe, and I honestly have never known anyone who tried it and didn't like it. By using this recipe you will get much the same effect as by making Hassenpfeffer, a very difficult classic German recipe for rabbit, with a tiny fraction of the time and effort.

1 or 2 rabbits cut in
  quarters
½ cup vinegar
2 teaspoons salt
1 tablespoon minced
  onion or 1 small onion,
  chopped

4 whole cloves
2 bay leaves
½ teaspoon allspice
  (optional)
½ cup dark raisins
¼ cup brown sugar

Place rabbit pieces in deep pot and cover with cool water. Add ¼ cup vinegar to water and bring to boil. Let boil for 10 minutes. THROW THIS WATER AWAY. Again, cover rabbit with cool water and add ¼ cup vinegar, 2 teaspoons salt, onion, cloves, bay leaves and allspice. Cook until almost tender and then add raisins and brown sugar. Continue cooking until rabbit is tender. This will be 1 hour, or possibly slightly longer. Remove rabbit from pot and thicken liquid with a paste of flour and water for gravy. I use ¼ cup flour and ¼ cup water. Replace rabbit in thickened gravy and heat just before serving.
[*Serves 4 to 6*]

KATHY McCORMICK'S RABBIT CASSEROLE

This recipe of Kathy's is somewhat more complicated than others. It's worth the extra time and trouble because it is so very good.

2 rabbits, cut in serving pieces
4 large onions
¼ cup butter
⅓ cup white vinegar
1 tablespoon sugar
4 slices stale white bread
  (day old at least)
Dijon mustard

2 sprigs parsley
¼ teaspoon dried thyme
Small bay leaf
1 quart dark beer
Salt and pepper

Preheat oven to 350° F. Brown rabbit and onions in butter using a skillet. Place onions in a large casserole along with vinegar and sugar. Place rabbit pieces on top. Spread bread slices with mustard and place alongside. Add parsley, thyme and bay leaf. Cover with beer, season with salt and pepper to taste. Cover casserole, cook for 1 ½ hours or until tender in oven. (Kathy says that if you have a friend who brews beer at home, ask for a bottle. This dish is especially good when both beer and bread are homemade.)
[*Serves 4 to 6*]

BAKED RABBIT IN BURGUNDY

Wine always seems to go especially well with game.
Therefore, you'll find this recipe is extremely tasty and
gets a fine reception from family and friends.

1 cup burgundy or other
　dry, red wine
2 tablespoons red wine
　vinegar
1 small onion, sliced
1 bay leaf
½ teaspoon each dried
　thyme and rosemary
4 peppercorns

1 rabbit cut in serving
　pieces
2 tablespoons vegetable or
　olive oil
Salt to taste

Combine wine, vinegar, onion, bay leaf, herbs and
peppercorns. Pour these over pieces of rabbit and
marinate for several hours. (Meanwhile you can go out
shopping or hunting for more rabbits!) Then remove
rabbit pieces and dry on paper toweling. Heat oil in
heavy skillet and brown rabbit pieces on all sides. Place
browned meat in casserole, and strain marinade before
pouring it over the meat. Add salt and cook covered in
a slow oven, about 300°F. for 1 to 1½ hours. After 40
minutes of cooking, add more wine if needed to cover
rabbit.
[*Serves 3 to 4*]

MICHIGAN RABBIT STEW

This might be a good place to mention that cottontail rabbit, snowshoe hares, and swamp and marsh rabbits may be used in any of these recipes. Jackrabbits are something else again. Look upon any wild rabbit weighing more than 5 pounds with deep suspicion. It's likely to be a jackrabbit and very tough.

1 rabbit, cut in serving pieces
1 teaspoon salt
3 tablespoons butter
1 cup potatoes, cut like French fries
½ cup celery, cut in strips
½ cup carrots, cut in strips
1 medium-size onion, sliced

2 cups broth (from rabbit)
1 8-ounce can tomato sauce
¼ cup parsley, chopped
Salt to taste

Cover rabbit with cool water to which 1 teaspoon of salt has been added. Simmer until rabbit is tender. Remove pieces and drain. SAVE BROTH. When cool, bone rabbit and cut into 1-inch pieces. Melt butter in skillet and add potatoes, celery, carrots and onion. Cover and cook 15 minutes. Add broth and tomato sauce. Bring this vegetable mix to a boil and add meat, parsley and salt to taste. Thicken with flour and water, and cook for another 15 minutes.

[*Serves 3 to 4*]

STEAMED RABBIT

This is one of the favorite recipes of Bill Satterfield's mother. Bill and his father go hunting together regularly. We all met at the time my husband was writing a daily newspaper column on hunting and fishing. Bill called him up to find out where he could get game near Fort Monmouth, New Jersey, where he was stationed. Since then, we've become good friends. The elder Satterfields live in Owensboro, Kentucky, a great place to visit, particularly if you enjoy quail and rabbit.

1 rabbit cut in serving   ⅓ cup shortening
   pieces   Salt to taste
½ teaspoon paprika
¾ cup flour

Soak rabbit pieces for at least 1 hour in salt water before cooking unless entire rabbit has already been soaked to remove blood. Drain and dry rabbit on paper towel. Mix paprika with flour in a paper bag. Place rabbit in bag and shake so all pieces are well dusted with flour. Sauté rabbit in shortening using heavy skillet until browned on all sides.

Drain off almost all shortening leaving about 1 tablespoon shortening in skillet. Add water to ½ inch depth in skillet and cover tightly with lid. Bring to simmer and cook until fork tender (about 1 hour). Add water as needed during cooking. Remove rabbit pieces to dish when tender. Add flour and water thickening to skillet drippings and scrapings to make gravy. Salt to taste, pour gravy over rabbit and serve.
[*Serves 4*]

HUNTER'S FAVORITE RABBIT

Mrs. J. Carter Day, Frances to her many friends, lives in a ranch-style home near Catlett, Virginia. For many years her husband has managed in Virginia one of the finest game preserves anywhere. This is her favorite recipe, and it is truly marvelous.

1 rabbit, cut in serving pieces	2 tablespoons dry mustard
1 teaspoon salt	1 teaspoon curry powder
1 clove garlic	1 teaspoon salt
Flour	¼ teaspoon pepper
	1 cup light cream

Boil rabbit pieces in water with salt and garlic until almost tender (at least 1 hour). Discard water and dry rabbit with paper towel. Dust rabbit with mixture of flour, dry mustard, curry powder and pepper. Heat oil in skillet and fry rabbit until golden brown. Add cream and cover skillet. Simmer until tender (approximately 1 hour).
[*Serves 4*]

FRIED RABBIT

This is probably an all-time basic recipe. You can use it with everything from a campfire or wood stove to a modern kitchen range. Cut rabbit into quarters or smaller pieces. Place pieces in a deep pot and cover with cool water to which ¼ cup of vinegar or 2 tablespoons of salt has been added. Bring to a boil and let boil for 10 minutes. This boiling is necessary to make the rabbit tender and remove a strong gamey taste. THROW

THIS WATER AWAY. Then start over. Cover game with cool water and add 1-2 teaspoons salt. Boil until almost tender. Remove pieces from water, dry on paper towel, and dip in seasoned corn meal or flour. Fry as you would chicken. Naturally, a young rabbit can be cooked more quickly than an older one. But the life span of a rabbit is so short (less than 2 years, whether hunted or not) that most every rabbit you cook will be relatively young.

RABBIT "CHICKEN" SALAD

If your family enjoys chicken salad, you can make something even better from rabbit. This is a wonderful way, in fact, in which to use any game leftovers you may have. The added flavor that game imparts, makes this "chicken" salad truly scrumptious.

2 cups cooked rabbit (or other game) cut in bite-size cubes
¼ cup French dressing
1 cup chopped celery
¼ cup mayonnaise
½ cup sour cream

2 hard-boiled eggs cut in eighths
2 tablespoons capers (optional)

Combine 2 cups of rabbit, chicken, squirrel, pheasant, or wild duck cubes with French dressing. Cover and let stand at least 1 hour. Add celery, mayonnaise and sour cream and mix well. Finally, add the hard-boiled eggs and capers and stir them in gently. Refrigerate until serving.
[*Serves 4*]

RABBIT IN BAG

This is an excellent recipe since the rabbit becomes tender without parboiling.

¼ cup flour
1 teaspoon salt
¼ teaspoon pepper
1 rabbit, quartered

½ cup onion, chopped
1 cup celery, sliced
2 tablespoons butter
½ cup dry red wine
½ teaspoon Kitchen
    Bouquet

Preheat oven to 350° F. Combine flour, salt and pepper in small size (10 x 16-inch) Brown-In-Bag. Add rabbit and shake gently to coat. Spread out rabbit pieces in bottom of bag. Add onion, celery and butter. Combine wine and Kitchen Bouquet; add to bag. Secure bag with twist-tie and make 6 ½-inch slits in top. Cook 1 hour or until tender. The sauce in the bag will be ready to spoon over the rabbit.
[*Serves 3 to 4*]

RABBIT IN PRESSURE COOKER

This outstanding recipe was developed by Merrill L. Petoskey, chief of the Wildlife Division in the Michigan Department of Natural Resources.

½ cup flour
2 teaspoons salt
¼ teaspoon pepper
2 or 3 rabbits, quartered
¼ cup butter or oil
¼ cup dry red wine
¼ cup water

2 cans condensed
    mushroom soup
2 onions, sliced
1 dash each of Tabasco
    and Worcestershire
    sauces
1 bay leaf

Place flour, 1 teaspoon salt and ¼ teaspoon pepper in a paper bag. Drop rabbit pieces into bag and shake until well coated. Melt fat in open pressure cooker and braise rabbit until golden brown. Add remaining ingredients including other teaspoon salt. Close pressure cooker and cook for 20 minutes at 15 pounds pressure. Cool cooker immediately.

[*Serves 6*]

Squirrel

People have asked me, "How can you eat a cute squirrel?" Obviously, they've never tried it. Nor would they consider squirrels "cute" if they ever had had any invade their attic. Of course, any animal can be considered "cute." For all I know a buzzard is perfectly darling — to another buzzard. Unlike buzzards, squirrels make wonderful table fare. Our forefathers considered these small animals their staff of life and hunted them all year. Of course I'm referring to grey squirrels and the even larger fox squirrels. Other species, including those noisy red squirrels, are too small.

You skin a squirrel about as you do a rabbit. I cut the skin at the nape of the neck, hold the head firmly in my left hand, and pull the skin off with my right hand. It's basically like peeling a banana. Then use your kitchen shears to remove head, paws, and tail.

SQUIRREL POT PIE FOR PRESSURE COOKER

This recipe was developed by Jo Lynn Seifert of Centreville, Virginia. Married to an avid hunter, Jo Lynn has started hunting too and particularly enjoys going afield for squirrel and pheasant.

2 squirrels, quartered
2 cups water
1 teaspoon salt
1 stalk celery, halved
1 cup peeled potatoes, cut in chunks
1 cup carrots, sliced

1 cup frozen corn kernels
2 cups frozen peas
1 large onion, diced
Salt to taste
2 9-inch pie crusts unbaked (you can either make these at home or buy them frozen.)

Place squirrel pieces in pressure cooker and add 2 cups of cool water, 1 teaspoon of salt and celery. Close pressure cooker and cook for 15-20 minutes at 15 pounds pressure (same as for chicken). Cool cooker at once. Remove squirrel pieces and allow to cool. SAVE BROTH. Remove squirrel meat from bone and cut into bite-size pieces. To the broth remaining in pressure cooker add potato chunks and sliced carrots. In closed pressure cooker cook 5 minutes. Immediately cool the cooker. Remove these cooked vegetables and add frozen corn, frozen peas and sliced onion to broth in pressure cooker. Close pressure cooker and cook for 1 minute. Again, cool cooker at once.

Add boned squirrel and ALL vegetables to broth; stir, and salt to taste. If liquid is needed, add water. If the mixture is too thin, thicken with flour. Finally, put one pie crust on bottom of casserole; add squirrel,

broth, and vegetables from pressure cooker; place second crust on top, and bake in 425°F. oven until crust is brown. Though this recipe may appear involved, it actually is quite easy to make.)
[*Serves 4*]

BRUNSWICK STEW

This is a traditional recipe, very popular at hunting camps since it's a simple hearty meal to prepare and is especially good with squirrel as its base.

2 squirrels, quartered	1 cup green lima beans
2 teaspoons salt	1 tablespoon sugar
1 can condensed tomato	Salt and pepper to taste
soup or 1 cup canned	1 cup canned
tomatoes	whole-kernel corn
1 onion, sliced thin	¼ pound butter
3 potatoes, sliced thin	

Place squirrel pieces in deep kettle with 2 teaspoons salt and cover with water. Simmer until tender (about 1½ hours). Remove squirrel pieces, debone the meat and cut into 1-inch pieces. Return meat to broth in kettle and add tomato soup (or stewed tomatoes), onion, potatoes, lima beans, sugar, and salt and pepper to taste. Cook until potatoes and beans are tender. Add corn and butter and cook additional 5 minutes.
[*Serves 4*]

FRIED SQUIRREL

This is similar to fried chicken. It tastes just as good.

Squirrels, in halves or quarters	Flour or corn meal
2 teaspoons salt	

Place squirrel pieces in deep pot, cover with cool water, add 2 teaspoons of salt, and boil until nearly tender. (Check after 1 hour.) Remove pieces from water, dry on paper towel, dust with flour or corn meal and fry exactly as you would chicken.

[*Allow ½ squirrel per person*]

SQUIRREL IN APPLE BAKE

This is one of Frances Day's enjoyable recipes. Mrs. Day delights in getting outdoors in the autumn woods and shooting squirrels. These results help justify her time spent afield.

2 squirrels, halved	3 tart apples, peeled and quartered
1 teaspoon salt	3 tablespoons honey
Flour	3 tablespoons brown sugar
¼ teaspoon pepper	
½ cup vegetable oil	

Preheat oven to 350°F. Boil squirrel pieces in water with 1 teaspoon of salt until tender. Save 1 cup of broth. Dry squirrel pieces on paper toweling; roll them in flour and pepper. Heat oil in skillet and fry squirrel until brown. Place browned pieces in a baking dish and add the 1 cup of broth you have saved. On top of squirrel pieces place the apple quarters and mixture of honey and brown sugar. Bake in oven about 45 minutes or until apples are done.

[*Serves 4*]

Woodchuck [Groundhog]

The woodchucks or groundhogs which gardeners and farmers hate are much sought after by hunters who enjoy pursuing an elusive quarry. Many states have a special summer season for these animals. (They hibernate all winter.) Since the animals eat nothing except green leafy vegetable matter, their meat is tasty. Unfortunately, they are very ugly animals, and many hunters would rather bury them than face the chore of skinning and cleaning. It's a mistake. Though woodchuck is more stringy than rabbit, it is quite good and well worth the time spent in preparation.

As I've discovered by experience, the best idea is to make the hunter skin and clean out his own woodchuck. It's quite a task. The skin, while not thick, is as tough as the hide of a rhinoceros and must make marvelous leather. Only the sharpest knife will pierce it. Quartering a groundhog calls for a hacksaw if a meat saw is not available. Bones and joints are extremely thick and strong, and your kitchen shears, so handy with rabbit, squirrel and game birds, cannot cope.

STEWED WOODCHUCK

The last woodchuck I cooked was killed and retrieved
for me by Bobby Blanc, our male Brittany. When I first
saw Bobby, I was alarmed that he had killed a pheasant.
Then I discovered he was proudly carrying a heavy
woodchuck. Somehow, he had shaken it to death,
because even his sharp teeth couldn't pierce the skin.
This is the recipe I used in preparing it.

½ cup vinegar
1 teaspoon salt

1 small onion, chopped or
1 tablespoon minced
onion flakes
4 whole cloves
2 bay leaves

Quarter woodchuck and remove and discard any fat
remaining on meat. Place quarters in a deep pot, cover
with cool water and ¼ cup vinegar, and bring to a boil.
Boil 10 minutes. THROW THIS WATER AWAY. This
boiling removes the gamey taste of woodchuck. Again
cover woodchuck quarters with cool water and ¼ cup
vinegar. Add all the other ingredients. Bring to a boil
and simmer until meat is tender in approximately 1 to
1 ½ hours, depending on size and age of animal.
Remove meat from pot and thicken remaining broth
with a paste of flour and water for gravy.
[*Serves 4*]

Muskrat

If you've ever been down South and eaten "marsh rabbit," it's probably been muskrat. There actually are both swamp rabbits and marsh rabbits, relatives of the familiar cottontail. But they are considered ordinary rabbit. Of course, there's no reason a muskrat shouldn't be delicious. He is not a rabbit, but a clean vegetarian and a daily bather.

MICHIGAN MUSKRAT

1 muskrat, skinned, disjointed and cut into suitable pieces
1 quart water
1 teaspoon salt
1/8 teaspoon pepper
1 small onion, sliced
½ cup melted butter or margarine
1 cup tomato catsup
½ teaspoon Worcestershire sauce

After washing and cutting your muskrat into quarters, or slightly smaller pieces, soak it overnight in a solution of 1 tablespoon salt to 1 quart water in order to remove the gamey flavor. When ready to cook, place your pieces of muskrat in a deep pot and add a fresh quart of water along with salt, pepper and onion. Cook for about 1 hour. Remove the pieces of muskrat from the water, dry on paper toweling and brown the meat with butter or margarine in a heavy skillet (or one lined with teflon if you prefer). After browning on one side, turn and immediately pour catsup and Worcestershire sauce over the meat. Almost cover the meat with water (this will take about 1 cup). Simmer until gravy is thick enough to serve after about 30 minutes.
[*Serves 3 to 4*]

Raccoon

If you live in the country and somebody offers you a small or medium-sized raccoon, be sure to take it. Raccoon tastes almost exactly the same as good roast pork, and it's not nearly as rich. To prepare for cooking, the raccoon should be cleaned out, skinned and ALL fat removed.

ROAST RACCOON WITH YAMS

1 small to medium-size raccoon
1 teaspoon salt
4 peppercorns
1 bay leaf
1 small onion, sliced, or ½ teaspoon dry, minced onion

2 apples, peeled, cored and quartered
3 yams, peeled and halved
1 teaspoon cinnamon
2 tablespoons brown sugar
1 ½ cups apple cider

Preheat oven to 350°F. Place entire raccoon in a deep pot. Add salt, peppercorns, bay leaf, and onion. Cover raccoon completely with cool water and bring to a boil. Then cover the pot and simmer until raccoon is almost tender. This will take approximately 30 minutes. Remove raccoon from pot and discard water.

Place raccoon in roasting pan, and arrange apples and yams around it. Sprinkle apples and yams with cinnamon and brown sugar. Add your cider and cook uncovered in oven until raccoon is brown. It will take about 30 minutes. Then cover roasting pan with lid and cook for 30 minutes additional. Baste twice with the cider during roasting process.

[*Serves 3 to 4*]

Beaver

Back in pioneer days roast beaver was considered a
delicacy. I found out why after trying one. Beaver has a
flavor much like that of prime veal.

ROAST BEAVER

1 small to medium-size
    beaver
Baking soda
Salt and pepper
1 medium onion, sliced

Preheat oven to 350°F. Remove all surface fat from
beaver and place in a deep roasting pan. Cover
completely with cool water to which 1 teaspoon of
baking soda has been added for each quart of water.
Bring to boil and boil 10 minutes before discarding
water. Then sprinkle beaver with salt and pepper and
cover with sliced onion. Add ½ cup water to roasting
pan, and be prepared to add more during cooking
process. Place in oven and roast uncovered for 30
minutes. Then cover roaster and continue to cook for
another 30 minutes or until beaver is very tender.
[*Serves 3 to 4*]

Rabbit or Small Game Dinner Menu

RABBIT [*or equivalent*]

BREAD DUMPLINGS

CARROT SOUFFLÉ

SPINACH SALAD

CHILLED ORANGE SLICES IN RED WINE

RAW APPLE CAKE

COFFEE

WINE, BURGUNDY OR ROSÉ

The recipes for all of these dishes are in the section on Accompaniments at the back of the book.

UPLAND GAME BIRDS

Ranging in size from a 6-ounce quail to a 20-pound wild turkey, upland game birds provide a considerable challenge, but are always a dependable culinary delight.

Of course, you don't have to go hunting to eat some of them. Pheasant and bob-white quail are often raised on special game farms and available at some supermarkets.

There are other ways of getting them too. A few years back, we lived in an area with plenty of wild pheasants. Naturally, I planned many pheasant dinner parties. One time with the last dinner only days away, I awoke to the terrible realization that we needed one more bird. And pheasant season was over. What to do?

Fate solved my problem very nicely. Following a night-long snow and sleet storm we managed to get our car down to the road so I might drive my husband to his commuter train. As we turned onto our rural road, I suddenly noticed a large cock pheasant lying with its feet in the air underneath the electric wires that ran along the road. It was obviously dead. "Look," I screeched. "Just what we need for dinner."

"For ptomaine, did you say, dear?" My husband asked wryly. He nevertheless leaped from the car, picked up the bird and found it to be warm. Watching to be sure nobody observed us, he stuffed it into the car trunk and slammed the lid.

At home a short while later as I unloaded the pheasant, I saw a burned area on the side of its neck. What evidently had happened was that a few hours before, at the height of the sleet, it had flown into the wires, touched more than one and electrocuted itself.

Our neighbors, who loved all wildlife, regularly sprinkled corn for the neighborhood pheasants and quail, and this bird was quite plump, actually fatter than any we had shot.

At dinner, one of our guests commented with pleasure that he hadn't found even one particle of shot in the plump pheasant. My husband never changed expression. "Joan's very careful what she serves," he observed.

I guess he thought that was the last laugh, but a few weeks later at the end of quail season his comeuppance came when our dog Meggie, weary of pointing a pheasant in an inpenetrable jungle of blackberry thorns, simply grabbed it and retrieved it right to his feet. Much to my hubby's surprise, the game warden failed to appear and arrest him, so we had rather a pheasant bonus. It wasn't as juicy and fat as "my" pheasant, however.

Although it may sound unusual, quite a few people who live in areas abounding in pheasant stop and retrieve those killed by cars. For some reason a pheasant will hide by the side of the road and emerge only as a car passes by. Some pheasant have caused serious accidents by breaking windshields.

Probably you'll get your own game birds the conventional way, via the hunting field. To prevent spoilage, birds should be field-dressed as soon as possible. This means the hunter should take a moment to slit the bird open below the breast and remove its insides. With pheasant, grouse, and other medium-size and large birds the livers should be retained. They are comparable to chicken liver. With quail, woodcock, dove and other small birds the liver is too small to bother with.

If the birds have not been dressed in the field, they should be at home the same day they arrive. As we've mentioned, all this talk about letting game hang, is nothing but medieval twaddle. The sooner a bird is drawn, plucked, and frozen or cooked the better it will taste.

Plucking upland birds is easy enough. With small birds you cut off the wings and feet with kitchen shears to save time and then simply pull out the feathers.

With pheasant, grouse, partridge, or prairie chicken, cut off the wings and feet with your shears, boil a kettle of water, let the water cool for about five minutes and then pour it over the bird which you've placed in the sink. Or, you can pour the hot water into a bucket or pot, and dunk your bird, using the head as a handle. Either way will loosen the feathers and they will come out easily.

Some people will tell you they skin pheasant and other game birds. It's not that much easier than plucking, and a skinned bird doesn't brown well so you're limited in the ways you can cook it. After plucking your bird, be sure to remove the crop and cut off the head. The crop is a small fleshy pouch at the lower end of the neck. A quick note on plucking: The best idea is to sit down comfortably in a chair and hold the bird inside the mouth of a large paper bag. Those in which the supermarket packs your groceries are first-rate. This method makes plucking a cinch and leaves no mess.

When plucking is completed, wash the bird out carefully in cold water, remove any blood, take out the lungs and discard any shot pellets you may find. Badly shot-up areas should be cut away. Finally, place the bird to drain on layers of paper towel.

With small birds take your kitchen shears and cut them up the backbone before washing and draining. This enables you to remove the lungs. After draining place each bird in a plastic sandwich bag. Large birds, which I'll come to further on, should be left whole.

The small birds in their individual sandwich bags are placed in a plastic storage bag which is snugly closed to make it airtight. These sandwich bags are a wonderful convenience. With them you can remove the exact number of birds you may need for any meal. Place a slip of paper in each bag indicating species and date frozen so you can use earliest game first. Put the paper slip in such a position so you needn't open the bag to read it. If faced by a wild turkey, don't despair. It will take you more hot water for plucking than a pheasant, but the feathers will come out easily. Pluck it over an empty garbage can for easy disposal.

Of course, with all large birds you should go over the plucked carcass after washing and draining to make certain it's as you want it. Place your hand in the body cavity and make sure that all the insides have been removed. Also, be sure to remove any shot you may see or feel and remove any blood clots. The best way to wash a large bird is to run cold water through the neck opening and out the main cavity opening.

Instead of using freezer paper or heavy duty foil, you may wrap larger birds in double plastic bags, one inside the other. The double thickness prevents a sharp bone from puncturing the bag and allowing air to enter which causes freezer burn.

In case you haven't read the Venison section, all game can be wrapped successfully with freezer paper or heavy duty aluminum foil, providing a drugstore fold is used along the center. If in doubt, see the diagram in the

Venison section. You can mark aluminum foil by writing on tape, and then affixing the tape to the foil.

Just remember to slit your small birds down the back before freezing and wash out large birds before freezing whole. For now, it's time we returned to the main purpose of this book: cooking.

Dove and Woodcock

These two birds have nothing in common except that similar recipes work well with both. If you live in the West, you can easily substitute band-tail pigeons or white-wing doves for the mourning doves I've used here. Also, I've found that domestic pigeons, so plentiful around barns and hated by many farmers, are good eating and can be cooked the same as doves. Of course, the younger birds are better if you can distinguish them, and pigeons, being larger, need more cooking than doves.

Woodcock, just like dove, are almost entirely dark meat. In fact the breasts are dark and the tiny legs are white meat, which makes them rather backwards, doesn't it? Never cook woodcock with any other species unless you want them all to have a woodcock flavor. Woodcock taste somewhat like liver and impart this flavor to anything cooked with them. I find them delicious, but if you dislike liver, you may not enjoy them too much.

Whenever I think of either doves or woodcock I recall our old Irish water spaniel, Haley McCool. She was the greatest dog and no matter who shot a bird, Haley always retrieved it and carried it to my husband. When dove hunting with friends, we often had a double limit before we fired more than a few shots!

I'll never forget the time in New Brunswick, Canada, when Haley decided to bring us a porcupine. Fortunately, we were able to find a veterinarian to remove the quills. As he dosed her with sodium pentothal, he inquired, "Now tell me, Haley, who bit who?" It took a few hours the next day before Haley could do much of anything. Her front end would try to go one way and her rear another. Our poor dog really had a terrible hangover. She looked at us with such sad red eyes we couldn't even laugh. But fresh air helped. What happened to the porcupine? I'm sure it simply shrugged and went on its way.

DOVE OR WOODCOCK CASSEROLE

12 dove or woodcock	2 carrots, chopped
Salt and pepper	Fresh parsley, chopped or
Flour	parsley flakes
⅓ cup butter or	1 cup chicken broth or
margarine	chicken bouillon
1 small onion, minced	½ cup dry, white wine

Preheat oven to 350°F. Split birds down the back, and add salt and pepper to flour before dusting birds lightly. Melt butter in heavy or Teflon-lined skillet and place birds within it breast side down. Sauté, turning frequently until browned on both sides. Remove birds from skillet and place within a lidded casserole. Pour drippings from skillet over birds, and add onion, carrots, parsley, chicken broth and wine. Cover and bake for 45 minutes. Spoon the wine gravy over the birds when serving.
[*Serves 4 to 5*]

SPAGHETTI WITH DOVES

This sounds unusual, but it's very good and comes from
Pat Auld down in Kerrville, Texas. As a change from
the usual sautéed doves, I recommend this recipe
highly.

3-4 tablespoons olive oil
6-8 doves
3 buds garlic
1 large onion, chopped
1 8-ounce can tomato
  sauce
1 small can tomato paste
  (with 2 or more cans
  of water)

1 bay leaf
Dried mushrooms
Salt and pepper
Grated Romano cheese

Add oil to deep skillet and brown doves quickly.
Remove birds and set aside. Add garlic and chopped
onion and fry until golden. Add tomato sauce and
tomato paste with 2 (or more) cans of water. Then add
bay leaf, mushrooms, and salt and pepper to taste.
Simmer and immediately add the doves. Then cook
slowly for two hours or longer until doves are tender.
Cook and drain spaghetti separately, mix with sauce
from doves and sprinkle with Romano cheese. Serve
doves with spaghetti on separate platters.
[*Allow 2 to 3 doves per person*]

SAUTÉED DOVE OR WOODCOCK

Split 10 or 12 birds down the back. Dust lightly with
flour. Melt ¼ cup (½ stick) of butter in a heavy or
Teflon-lined skillet. Brown doves quickly on skin side,
turn and cook on bone side and turn again. Reduce
heat and continue cooking until birds are done in about
15 or 20 minutes. After sprinkling birds with salt add
5 tablespoons of Madeira wine to the drippings in the
skillet. Stir well and spoon mixture over birds when
serving.
[*Allow 3 doves or 2 to 3 woodcock per person*]

ROAST WOODCOCK

For some reason, you don't hear much about woodcock
except in New England and Canada's maritime
provinces. One reason must be that this migratory
species doesn't ordinarily linger long in any one place
on its journey to wintering grounds in Louisiana.
However, they are found as far west as Minnesota and in
every state east of the Mississippi River. Wherever you
happen to meet up with woodcock, this recipe works
extremely well.

   Split the desired number of birds up the back and
place them in a shallow baking pan. Place the pan in a
preheated 400°F. oven and roast for 15 to 20 minutes.
While roasting, baste twice with melted butter to which
a small amount of dry red wine has been added. Then
add salt and pepper to taste and serve on toast.
[*Allow 2 to 3 woodcock per person*]

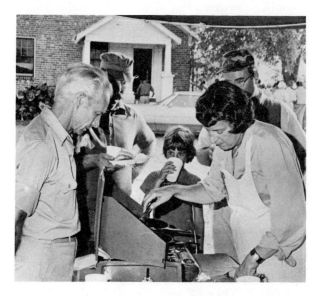

Joan Cone prepares Sautéed Doves for hungry hunters
at the Annual Invitational Dove Hunt at Curles Neck
Farm near Richmond, Virginia. Many of Mrs. Cone's
recipes can be used outdoors on camping stoves.

DOVE BREASTS STROGANOFF

Here's another Pat Auld dove recipe which works well.
It's based on the fact that some people prefer to dress
doves by simply snapping out the breasts and
discarding everything else. To be candid I feel this is
wasteful. Yet it's true there's not much else to eat on a
dove except the breasts. Besides, the recipe is superb.

12 to 18 whole dove
  breasts
1 medium onion, diced
1 can condensed cream of
  celery soup
1 4-ounce can of
  mushrooms
½ cup sauterne

Oregano, rosemary, salt
  and pepper to taste
2 teaspoons Kitchen
  Bouquet (or
  equivalent for color)
1 cup sour cream

Preheat oven to 325°F. Place breasts in large baking
dish. Do not crowd them. Sauté onion in skillet and
add remaining ingredients except sour cream. Mix and
pour over birds in baking dish. Cover baking dish
lightly and bake for 1 hour, turning breasts
occasionally. Then add sour cream and stir. Bake
uncovered for 20 minutes. Serve over rice. Brown rice,
or a mixture of white and wild rice, is especially good.
[*Serves 6*]

Quail

There's an old saying to the effect that "sportsmanship is inversely proportionate to the size of the game." This means that quail hunting is very sporting indeed. Particularly in the Confederate states quail are the gentleman's game. Huge tracts of land are managed especially for them; breeds of dog, notably the English pointer, are developed to seek them out; and clothing, shotguns and much other gear is made especially for the men and women who go afield in search of the elusive bob-white. There are other quail in the West. Mountain, valley, harlequin, and scaled quail are found beyond the continental divide. They are difficult birds to cope with in the field, but just as good as a bob-white in the pan.

SAUTÉED QUAIL

Split 6-8 birds down the backs. Dust lightly with flour. Melt ¼ cup (½ stick) butter in a heavy or Teflon-lined skillet. Brown quail quickly on skin side, turn and cook on bone side. Then turn again. Reduce heat and continue cooking until birds are tender in about 25 or 30 minutes. Sprinkle birds with salt and remove from skillet. Add ½ cup dry, white wine to drippings in skillet. Bring to boil and spoon over quail when serving.
[*Allow 2 quail per person*]

QUAIL CASSEROLE

Here's an easy recipe that's very good when you're having another couple or two for dinner. As it takes 1 hour in the oven, you can place it there just when the doorbell rings and enjoy cocktails with your company.

8-12 quail
Salt
Flour
⅓ cup butter or
    margarine

½ pound fresh
    mushrooms or
    1 4-ounce can sliced
    mushrooms
Fresh parsley, chopped or
    parsley flakes
2 cups dry white wine

Preheat oven to 350°F. Split birds down back. Add salt to flour and dust lightly. Melt butter in skillet and place birds skin side down. Sauté until browned on both sides. Remove birds from skillet and place them in a casserole with lid. Add mushrooms and parsley and pour enough wine into casserole to half cover the birds. Cover and place in oven for 1 hour. Spoon the clear wine gravy over the birds.

[*Serves 4 to 6*]

Kitchen shears are an essential cooking tool in preparing game. Joan Cone uses them here to split quail backs for a casserole.

QUAIL IN BAG

Yes, I like oven cooking bags for quail. The birds stay juicy and tasty, the gravy makes itself, and clean-up is minimal. How can you beat these advantages?

1 tablespoon flour
½ cup dry, white wine
½ teaspoon Kitchen Bouquet (for color)

2 stalks celery, coarsely chopped
1 2-ounce can sliced mushrooms (reserve liquid)
6 quail
Butter or margarine, melted
Salt

Preheat oven to 350°F. Shake 1 tablespoon flour into small size (10 x 16-inch) Brown-In-Bag, and place in 2-inch deep roasting pan. Combine wine and Kitchen Bouquet. Pour this into bag and stir until well mixed with flour. Add celery and mushrooms with liquid. Brush quail with melted butter and sprinkle with salt. Place quail atop vegetables within bag. Close bag with twist tie and make 6 ½-inch slits in top. Cook for 1 hour. You will find a perfect gravy in the bag. Spoon this over the quail while serving.
[*Allow 2 quail per person*]

OVEN BROWNED QUAIL

This recipe comes from Mrs. W.F. Satterfield in Owensboro, Kentucky, whose family, as I've mentioned, eats a great deal of quail. Having used her recipe regularly, I can understand its popularity at her house.

8 quail	Flour
Salt	1 teaspoon Kitchen
Paprika	Bouquet
4 tablespoons butter	

Preheat oven to 350°F. Split quail down back. Cover quail with water in pan, add salt as desired, and boil until tender about 1½ to 2 hours. Save the broth. Remove birds and place breast side up in baking dish. Sprinkle breasts with paprika. Add 4 tablespoons of butter to 2 or 3 cups of broth. Gradually thicken this broth with a flour and water paste until gravy results. Add Kitchen Bouquet for color and salt to taste. Pour gravy over birds in baking dish, and bake in oven until gravy boils and bubbles (about 30 minutes). Baste birds 2 or 3 times with gravy during this baking period.
[*Serves 4*]

BROILED OR GRILLED QUAIL

Here's a great recipe to use in a camper or over a campfire, barbecue, Coleman stove or portable grill. All you do is split the bird down the back, brown breast side lightly and quickly in your skillet, then turn. Baste breasts liberally with melted butter or margarine. Cook 30 minutes or until tender. Salt and pepper to taste. [*Allow 2 quail per person*]

HUNTER'S QUAIL

This one is only slightly more sophisticated and everyone likes it.

4 quail	1 can condensed
Salt and pepper	consommé
¼ cup butter	Pinch of thyme
2 tablespoons flour	½ bay leaf
	½ cup dry, white wine

Split quail down back. Sprinkle birds with salt and pepper. Melt butter in skillet and brown quail slowly on both sides over medium heat. Sprinkle birds with flour, add remaining ingredients and cover skillet tightly. Simmer for 40 minutes or until quail are tender. Spoon pan juices over quail when serving.

[*Serves 2*]

Quail, Dove, Woodcock Dinner Menu

QUAIL [*or equilavent*]

WILD RICE [*Packaged mix*]

ARTICHOKE HEARTS AND SPINACH SOUFFLÉ

PINEAPPLE BAKE

PEACH CHUTNEY

PUMPKIN PIE IN NO-ROLL PASTRY SHELL

COFFEE

WINE, DRY WHITE

See the Accompaniments section at the back of the book for each recipe.

Partridge and Grouse

These birds are the tastiest you ever ate. They are larger than quail yet smaller than pheasant. You can use them in any of the quail or pheasant recipes in this book, but I thought you might like to try a few designed especially for these medium-size gamebirds. Whether you use ruffed grouse, sharp-tail grouse, prairie chicken, chukar partridge or Hungarian partridge will make very little difference. (Prairie chickens are almost as large as pheasants, and sage grouse can reach the size of small turkeys.) My only reservation is that spruce grouse and sage grouse because of their diet, which consists largely of spruce needles and sagebrush, are not especially good at times. The former are apt to taste like turpentine, and the latter . . . well, a very young one could be palatable but it seems a waste to shoot even at a large, mature bird of this species. All other grouse and partridge are consistently a gourmet delight.

BAKED PARTRIDGE IN BAG

Oven bags insure that rather dry game birds are moist and juicy when served.

1 tablespoon flour	Stuffing or ¼ orange for
½ cup dry, white wine	each bird
Salt	Melted butter or
2 partridges or grouse	margarine

Preheat oven to 350°F. Shake 1 tablespoon flour in small size (10 x 16-inch) oven cooking bag and place in a 2-inch deep roasting pan. Pour wine into bag and stir until well mixed with flour. Salt birds inside and out. Add either stuffing or ¼ orange in each bird's body cavity. If you stuff the bird, skewer or sew the opening shut. Brush entire surface of birds with melted butter and place inside bag. Close bag with twist tie and make 6 ½-inch slits in top. Cook for 1 hour. Remove birds from bag and serve with wine gravy remaining inside bag.

[*Serves 2*]

BAKED PARTRIDGE IN FOIL

This is the kind of recipe that makes your family and friends gnaw at the bones until absolutely nothing else remains.

2 to 4 partridges	½ to 1 cup dry, white
Stuffing, or ¼ orange	wine (depends on
for each bird	number of birds)
Melted butter or	
margarine	

Preheat oven to 425°F. Salt partridges inside and out. Either stuff with your favorite stuffing or place a quarter of an orange in the body cavity. Brush entire bird with melted butter. Place each bird on a piece of heavy-duty aluminum foil. Bring edges together and seal tightly. Place birds in shallow roasting pan and bake for 45 minutes. Open foil and allow birds to brown for another 15 minutes. Remove birds and foil from pan and add wine to drippings. Heat this liquid to boiling and serve as gravy.

[*Serve 1 bird per person*]

CHUKAR PARTRIDGE STUFFING

This is very good with chukar partridge, a popular
shooting preserve bird in many areas, and found wild in
desolate, dry, western areas which support almost
nothing else. Many states tried for years to introduce
chukars with no success whatever. Then somehow a few
got loose in the arid mountains of Nevada and
multiplied successfully. Originally they come from arid
mountains in Afghanistan and northern India and can
live in the wild only under similar surroundings.
Hungarian partridges are quite different except in size.
They are plains and wheatfield birds and capable of
feeding themselves even in deep snow. Introduced from
Europe, they are doing well in some areas, especially
the Canadian Provinces of Saskatchewan and Alberta.

1 tablespoon onion,
    minced
¼ cup butter or
    margarine

1 cup soft stale
    breadcrumbs
¼ teaspoon salt
Dash of pepper
½ cup raisins
½ cup pecans or walnuts,
    chopped

Sauté minced onion in butter or margarine until
tender. Add bread crumbs, salt and pepper. Brown the
crumbs lightly. Add raisins and nuts. Toss together
adding just a little water to moisten.
[*Fills any 1-pound bird*]

PARTRIDGE SOUP WITH DUMPLINGS

This recipe was very generously sent me by Mrs. Jean M.
Player of Eganville, Ontario. It's rather like
coq au vin without the ''vin,'' and is absolutely
delicious, much better than anything similar you may
have tried with ordinary chicken.

1 partridge (or grouse)   Water
   cut in serving pieces   Salt and pepper to taste
2 teaspoons summer
  savory
2 onions, chopped
1 ½ carrots, sliced
1 ½ teaspoons butter

Place first 5 ingredients in a deep pot and add enough
water to cover. Simmer for about 2 hours or until bird is
tender. Add salt and pepper to taste. Prepare the
following dumplings about 20 minutes before you are
ready to serve.
[*Serves 3 to 4*]

DUMPLINGS

1 cup flour   1 tablespoon shortening
2 teaspoons baking powder   ½ cup milk
¼ teaspoon salt

Place all ingredients in a small bowl and mix with a
fork. Drop teaspoonfuls into boiling soup. Cover and
boil for 10 to 15 minutes or until dumplings are done.
[*Serves 3 to 4*]

SAUTÉED RUFFED GROUSE

The most difficult thing about this recipe is obtaining the birds. Ruffed grouse are wary, tricky and have a knack of putting a tree between themselves and a load of birdshot.

4 grouse or partridge breasts, split	4 tablespoons butter
½ cup flour	¼ cup dry, white wine
	Salt

Dust grouse breasts in flour. Melt butter in skillet and slowly sauté breasts in butter over low heat until crisp and brown, taking about 12 to 15 minutes on each side. Salt breasts and remove from skillet. Add wine to drippings and bring to boil. Serve this clear gravy over birds.

[*Serves 4*]

PHEASANT

A major problem with pheasant has been that this delectable bird has a tendency to become extremely dry and tough when cooked like chicken. All my pheasant recipes take this into account and result in a pheasant that tastes like a game bird and is good to eat. Many old-time recipes use bacon strips in cooking pheasant. For example, a roast pheasant would have bacon strips attached to the breast with toothpicks. These recipes are used by many people even today, yet I'm sure they don't get much eating from their pheasant's legs. In addition, while I'm very fond of bacon, I prefer my pheasant to taste birdlike rather than porklike. And given today's big problems with cholesterol and fats, it seems smarter to hold the fat content of game meals to a minimum. While larding game with bacon was an excellent idea in its day, and still is if you're cooking under primitive conditions, nowadays we can do better and have fewer calories in the bargain.

PHEASANT CASSEROLE

Salt
Flour
1 pheasant, quartered
¼ cup butter or
    margarine

½ pound fresh
    mushrooms or
    1 4-ounce can sliced
    mushrooms
Parsley, fresh or dried
1 cup dry, white wine

Add salt to flour and dust pheasant quarters lightly. Melt butter in skillet and place pieces skin side down. Sauté until brown on both sides. Remove pheasant quarters from skillet and place them in a casserole with cover. Pour drippings from skillet over pheasant and add mushrooms and parsley. Pour wine into casserole until pheasant pieces are half covered. Cover and place in 350°F. oven for 1¼ hours or until tender. Baste with liquid in casserole several times during cooking. Spoon the clear gravy over the pheasant pieces when serving. [*Serves 3 to 4*]

PHEASANT IN SOUR CREAM SAUCE [For Pressure Cooker]

Where would we be without the pressure cooker? It saves so much time and cooks so well. I find it hard to get along without mine. Here's a tasty recipe that cuts your cooking time by more than half.

2 pheasants, quartered
Flour
3 tablespoons shortening
1 large onion, chopped
1 4-ounce can sliced
   mushrooms (reserve
   liquid)
Salt and pepper

2 cups dairy sour cream
¼ cup parsley, chopped
   (optional)

Wash and dry pheasant quarters and dredge lightly in flour. Heat pressure cooker, add shortening, brown meat well on all sides. Remove cooker from heat. Add onions, ½ cup of liquid drained from mushrooms (adding water if needed) and season with salt and pepper. Close cover securely, place pressure at 15 pounds and cook for 15 minutes (or use pressure and time indicated for chicken on your own pressure cooker). Cool cooker at once. Combine sour cream, mushrooms and parsley, then pour over meat. Simmer, (do not boil) for another 10 minutes without cover. [*Serves 6 to 8*]

PHEASANT IN CREAM SAUCE

Actually, this is Bill Satterfield's recipe and it is so very good I asked him if I could include it here.
You'll find it quite different from the preceding recipes, a good illustration that variety in cooking is truly the spice of life.

1 pheasant, quartered
Salt

1 can condensed cream of
    mushroom soup
½ cup dairy sour cream
1 4-ounce can sliced
    mushrooms, drained
¼ cup grated Parmesan
    cheese
¼ cup onion, chopped

Preheat oven to 350°F. Rub pheasant quarters with salt and place them in baking dish with skin side up. In separate bowl mix together the mushroom soup, sour cream, mushrooms, cheese and onion. Spread this mixture over the pheasant and bake in oven for 1 ½ to 2 hours or until tender. Baste occasionally with sauce during baking. Serve with oven-baked orange rice or wild rice mixture.
[*Serves 3 to 4*]

EASY PHEASANT

The only difficult part about this recipe is getting the pheasant. My husband claims that Izaak Walton's recipe for a trout dinner begins, "First catch your trout." A pheasant dinner faces the same problem.

Some years ago we were hunting alongside very dense woods. One of our dogs dashed into the brush and brambles, and we stopped, waited and tried to decide whether or not to follow. I noticed my husband pointing in the general direction of my feet. When I looked down, there was a pheasant strolling right up to me as if ready to say, "Hiya doing?"

Naturally, I wasn't about to shoot it on the ground. After all, it's not sportsmanlike. Besides, at that range, there'd be nothing left of the pheasant. Finally, I moved and the pheasant then noticed me and flew away, giving me a horse-laugh as only a cock pheasant can. (Cock pheasants make a raucous, horse-laugh cry when flushed. Supposedly, this is how they warn the hen pheasants of danger.)

Bringing up my gun, I squeezed the trigger, pulled the trigger, yanked the trigger. Absolutely nothing happened. In the excitement I had completely forgotten to click the safety off. You can imagine how my husband laughed and how red my face became. But, let's assume you have done better, and we'll get cooking.

2 pheasants, quartered	1 can condensed cream of
Flour	chicken soup
Salt and pepper	1 cup milk
½ cup butter	

Preheat oven to 350°F. Dredge pheasant pieces in flour

to which salt and pepper have been added. Melt butter in a heavy skillet (or Teflon-lined if you prefer) and brown pheasant pieces on both sides. Remove pheasant from skillet and place in a large baking dish or pan. Add soup and milk to drippings in the skillet and mix well over low heat. Pour this mixutre over the pheasant pieces. Cover and bake for 1 ¼ hours, or until pheasant pieces are tender. Spoon liquid over pheasant when serving.

[*Serves 6 to 8*]

PHEASANT IN CIDER

In Pennsylvania pheasant season and apple cider season generally come together. It's a great combination as this recipe proves.

¼ cup butter	2 cooking apples, peeled, cored, and quartered
1 pheasant, quartered	2 teaspoons cinnamon
	2 cups apple cider
	Salt to taste

Melt butter in your favorite skillet and brown the pheasant pieces on both sides. Add apples, cinnamon and cider. Salt to suit your personal taste. Place a cover over the skillet and simmer for 1 ¼ hours or until pheasant is tender.

[*Serves 3 to 4*]

BAKED PHEASANT IN BAG

To tell the truth, I find this the easiest way to serve a
single pheasant. No muss, no fuss, a wonderful meal.
What more could any cook ask for?

1 tablespoon flour	Melted butter or
½ cup dry white wine	margarine
Salt	Spice Parisienne
1 pheasant	(optional, use
	sparingly)
	½ orange

Preheat oven to 350°F. Shake 1 tablespoon flour in
small size (10 x 16-inch) oven cooking bag. Place bag in
2-inch deep roasting pan. Pour wine into bag and mix
well with flour. Salt inside body cavity of pheasant.
Brush outside of bird with melted butter and sprinkle
with seasoning. Stuff ½ orange into body cavity.
Then place pheasant in bag and close with twist tie.
Make 6 ½-inch slits in top of bag and cook for 1 ½
hours in oven. Before serving, carve pheasant into
quarters and use juice remaining in bag as gravy.
[*Serves 4*]

BAKED PHEASANT IN FOIL

This recipe is similar to the one before except for the oven temperature. If you don't have an oven bag handy, this alternate method makes a fine baked pheasant.

1 pheasant	½ orange
Salt	½ cup dry, white wine
Melted butter or margarine	
Spice Parisienne (optional, use sparingly)	

Preheat oven to 425°F. Sprinkle salt inside pheasant body cavity. Brush entire outer surface of bird with melted butter and sprinkle with salt and a very small amount of spice Parisienne. Stuff ½ orange into body cavity and place bird on heavy-duty aluminum foil. Bring edges of foil together and seal tightly. Place on a shallow roasting pan and bake for 1¼ hours. Open foil and allow pheasant to brown for another 15 minutes. Remove pheasant and foil from pan and add wine to the drippings which remain. Heat these to boiling. Carve pheasant into quarters (kitchen shears will be handy for this) and serve with the clear wine gravy. [*Serves 3 to 4*]

PHEASANT AU VIN

Back in the 16th century, a male chauvinist named Robert Burton coined the phrase, "Wine and women go together." He went on to explain that to him they both were plagues. If he'd had more sense and less malice, the expression might have come out as "wine and pheasant go together." It's true and the resultant is delightful.

2 pheasants, quartered	1 cup dry, white wine
⅓ cup butter or margarine	2 tablespoons lemon juice
1 cup sliced fresh mushrooms	¼ cup green onions, chopped
	1 teaspoon salt

Sauté pheasant in butter in your heavy or teflon skillet until browned on all sides. Remove pheasant pieces and sauté mushrooms in same butter for 10 minutes. Return pheasant to skillet and add all other ingredients. Cover and simmer for 1¼ hours or until tender.
[*Serves 6 to 8*]

Pheasant or Partridge Dinner Menu

PHEASANT [or partridge, grouse]

AVOCADO HALVES WITH FRENCH DRESSING

OVEN BAKED ORANGE RICE

BRUSSELS SPROUTS ORIENTAL

WHOLE CRANBERRY SAUCE

DROP BISCUITS

CHEESE CAKE

COFFEE

WINE, DRY WHITE

Recipes for all accompaniments are in section at the end of the book.

Wild Turkey

One of the most successful restoration projects of all times has been the wild turkey. Considered almost extinct in the 1930s, this wonderful bird is now relatively abundant in all its former range areas which have not been pre-empted by human populations. Interestingly enough, it was discovered that ''tame'' wild turkeys cannot be used to restock an area. The only system that works is to livetrap birds from existing wild flocks and move them to an appropriate new home.

There are a couple of things to consider with wild turkey. First of all, the gobbler season comes in springtime. Therefore, if you want a wild turkey for Thanksgiving or Christmas it will have to be very carefully frozen to last six months. You will also find some gobblers have a spongy material in their breasts. This is a form of protein which they form to use in place of eating during the mating season. While it's very nutritious, you'll find it too watery for cooking and it should be cut away when the bird is dressed.

Cook a wild turkey exactly the same as the supermarket variety. I suggest keeping the stuffing simple and going easy on seasoning. If you roast turkeys in aluminum foil, you can follow the exact directions which come with the heavy-duty foil. Personally, I've come around to using turkey-size oven cooking bags. As I've mentioned, they really work super-well with game because they retain the moisture so well.

Now, here's a recipe which doesn't involve any of these modern conveniences. It is simple, easy, and can be handled as well on a wood or coal stove as with a modern electric or gas range. The only problem is time. With a 15-pound wild turkey, you can spend the better part of a day in the kitchen. If it's a cold day, that might not be too bad.

ROAST WILD TURKEY — OPEN PAN METHOD

Preheat your oven to 325°F. Stuff turkey with any favorite stuffing. Brush the entire bird with melted butter or margarine and sprinkle with salt and pepper. Place turkey on a rack in an adequately sized roasting pan. All you do then is roast, allowing 22 to 25 minutes a pound. Baste the turkey often with equal parts of melted butter and dry white wine. A wild turkey has little fat and will be dry without the extra liquid. The low heat also protects your turkey from drying out. And with the wine and other liquids around, you'll probably have a wonderful time cooking it. Besides, wine enhances the flavor of game. Serve the turkey with your traditional accompaniments for the domestic bird or try some new recipes I've included in this book. [*Allow 1 pound per person*]

CORN BREAD DRESSING

Although you can use very complicated recipes for turkey stuffing, this one is both tasty and simple. It seems to go especially well with wild turkey.

6 cups crumbled corn bread
6 cups dry bread cubes
2 teaspoons salt
½ teaspoon pepper
1 ½ teaspoon poultry seasoning
½ cup butter or margarine
1 cup nutmeats, chopped
½ cup shortening
1 cup celery, diced
½ cup onion, chopped
2 eggs, beaten
1 ¼ cups water

Combine corn bread, bread cubes, salt, pepper and poultry seasoning in a large bowl. Cut butter into very small pieces, add it to corn bread mixture. Brown nutmeats in hot shortening, add celery and onion. Cook about 5 minutes until tender, and add this to corn bread mixture. Gradually add eggs and water while tossing lightly. You may wish to use an additional ¼ cup water if you prefer a more moist dressing. [*When lightly stuffed into body cavity and neck region, this mix is sufficient stuffing for a 12-pound turkey*]

WATERFOWL

It was George Orwell who wrote in *Animal Farm* the wonderful words, "All animals are equal, but some are more equal than others." He wasn't referring to waterfowl, but he should have been. When it comes to eating them, especially the various wild duck species, some are certainly much tastier than others.

Today, you have to be able to identify your birds or risk paying a substantial fine to state and federal wardens. Certain species, either because of nesting problems, disease or other complicated reasons, are not permitted to be shot at all. Others are so plentiful the hunter is encouraged by law to take bonus birds.

While you, as a cook, aren't expected to know all the fine points of identification, there are some general rules you must consider before cooking any waterfowl. The first question to ask yourself is very logical. After all, you'd better know, "What is it?" If you're in doubt, ask your family provider. Should a friend have dropped by and left the ducks, give him a phone call.

Why all this insistence? I'd better explain that there are some waterfowl species which are perfectly legal to hunt yet practically inedible, at least to our civilized tastes. So let's try and divide all the waterfowl tribes into some sort of fashion before we even think of beginning to cook them.

All geese are excellent. Brant, Canadas in several subspecies, snow geese, blue geese, and specklebellies make excellent table fare. Oh, once in a while you will encounter a tough old bird, or one that has feasted on bay cabbage with resultant poor odor and flavor. These

are rare exceptions to the general rule that goose
is great.

Ducks are divided into several categories. Most early
season ducks are puddle ducks: mallards, black duck,
pintails, widgeon, teal and wood duck. All of them are
excellent. Diving ducks usually arrive later, because
they live in deeper water which freezes later in the
season. Some diving ducks such as canvasbacks and
redheads are exceedingly good. As this book is written
they are scarce and protected, largely because their
nesting grounds have been pre-empted by agriculture.
Others, golden-eye, scaup, and old squaws, for
example aren't quite so good.

Sea ducks, including all the coots and scoters, along
with eider duck and harlequins, are mostly fish eaters.
If you want to remove the breasts, marinate them
thoroughly and hope to remove the fishy flavor.
Whether it's worth the effort depends on your taste
buds. Honestly, I hate to see any game wasted and I *try*
with these too.

Any duck with a serrated bill (like sawteeth) is a
merganser. It's pretty but totally inedible. Don't even
try to cook it.

Some people include the various railbird species
among waterfowl. Clapper rail, Virginia rail, and sora
rail are delicious. Follow the recipes for quail and you
won't go wrong. There's another rail-like bird, only
larger, known as a mudhen or coot. This isn't the same
''coot'' mentioned among the seaducks. It's not black
but grey with a white bill. It too should be cooked like
an upland gamebird. (But skin the mudhen instead of
plucking it and remove all fat.)

Despite anything you may hear, plucking waterfowl
is an arduous chore. Best idea by far is get someone else

to do it for you. As I mentioned in the introduction, this is possible in most areas catering to duck hunters where local residents will do it for a fee. If you have to do the job yourself, the paraffin method works reasonably well.

First, remove legs and wings. Then heat a bucket of water to almost boiling and dissolve two cakes of paraffin in it. Lower your waterfowl into this steaming mixture, slosh it about, and then remove your bird and let it cool.

When the paraffin has set, take a knife and slice the paraffin up the breast of the bird. Do not cut the bird's skin. Now you can yank off the feathers. Because the wax holds the feathers together, they come off en masse. You'll find quite often that you'll have to dip the bird a second time to do the job completely. As I said, it's work!

The only alternative is to just pluck away. You'll be amazed at how many feathers a duck or goose has, sometimes in a layer several inches thick.

If you're smart, you'll never pluck waterfowl in your kitchen unless you use the paraffin method. The reason is the down floats all over the place and into every room in your house.

Yes, there is an alternative. I haven't seen it advertised lately, though. At one time you could buy an attachment much like a paint mixer that would fit on a ¼-inch electric drill. It worked by getting under the feathers and literally whipping them off. For a while it rains feathers and down, but the end result is a clean goose or duck.

By now, you're probably scared almost silly at the thought of plucking waterfowl. I've made it sound worse than it really is, because, to be perfectly candid, I personally hate to do it. So let's get down to something much more enjoyable — cooking and eating wild duck.

Wild Duck

A few words of advice. Wild ducks are much easier to cook than the Long Island variety. They have less fat and don't have to be pricked constantly while cooking. This in turn means less grease in your oven.

WILD DUCK IN BAG

This method eliminates oven cleaning, a strong plus, and results in a roast duck which is really first-rate.

1 tablespoon flour	1 wild duck
½ cup orange juice	Melted butter or
¼ cup dry, white wine	margarine
	Salt
	½ apple

Preheat oven to 350°F. Shake 1 tablespoon flour in small size (10 x 16-inch) oven cooking bag and place in 2-inch deep roasting pan. Pour orange juice and wine into bag and stir until flour is well mixed with liquids. Brush duck with melted butter and sprinkle duck with salt all over, including within body cavity. Place apple within cavity and put duck into bag. Close bag with twist tie and make 6 ½-inch slits in top. Cook for 1 ½ hours or until tender.
[*Serves 2*]

BAKED WILD DUCK BREASTS

This duck breast recipe is especially recommended with the diving ducks. You can ordinarily figure that mallards and other puddle ducks are best roasted whole, and that divers are just as good or better if you discard all but the breasts. Arrange your breasts in a foil-lined pan and sprinkle with salt and pepper. Bake in a 375°F. oven for 40 minutes, basting occasionally with melted butter and dry, white wine. Remove breasts to serving platter. Pour drippings into a saucepan and remove all but a little of the fat. Add water and bring fat-free drippings to a boil. Thicken with a paste of flour and water. Add seasoning to taste and serve gravy over breasts.

[*One duck will feed 2 average appetites, or 1 hungry hunter*]

WILD DUCK — QUICK ROASTING METHOD

If you prefer to use a hot oven, here's a cooking method you'll want to try. All you do is place several orange slices within the empty body cavity of each duck. Put your ducks on a rack in a shallow pan and roast in a 450-475°F. oven. Baste ducks often and generously with melted butter and dry, red wine. You can substitute orange juice for the wine, if you prefer. Roast for 20-30 minutes and add salt and pepper to taste. Discard orange slices and serve with pan juices.

[*One wild duck yields 2 servings*]

WILD DUCK — SLOW ROASTING METHOD

This is a bit more complicated than the recipe preceding. You will find it worth the effort in savory roast duck. There's no doubt that slow roasting will tend to keep your ducks moist. You'll probably want to experiment until you find the type of recipe which works best with your equipment and for your personal tastes.

4 wild ducks   Melted butter
2 apples, sliced   Dry, white wine
½ teaspoon salt
Dash of nutmeg

Preheat oven to 350°F. Stuff each duck with apple slices, ½ teaspoon salt, and a dash of nutmeg. Place ducks upon a rack in a shallow pan and roast in oven. Baste often and generously with melted butter and wine. Roast for 1 hour or 1½ hours until birds are done (It may take longer depending on size and age of ducks.) Discard apple slices, and serve with pan juices as gravy. One duck will serve two.
[*Serves 8*]

WILD DUCK IN SKILLET

Some people prefer to simply cut off and skin the breasts of all wild ducks in preference to plucking and cooking the entire bird. This isn't as wasteful as it might appear because there is almost nothing else to eat on a wild waterfowl.

1 or 2 ducks, quartered
   or 2 to 4 duck breasts
4 tablespoons butter
2 tablespoons flour

1 cup red wine
2 cups beef broth
Salt and pepper to taste
2 small onions, thinly
   sliced
1 bay leaf
2 cloves
Parsley, chopped

Brown the duck pieces in butter in a skillet. Transfer duck to a deep pot or casserole. Add flour to the skillet and brown it well in the butter. Gradually stir in wine, broth, salt and pepper, onions, bay leaf and cloves. Bring to a boil and simmer 5 minutes stirring frequently. Pour this sauce over the duck breasts, cover the pot or casserole, and simmer for 1½ hours or until tender. Add chopped parsley. If the sauce is too thin, you should thicken with a paste of flour and water. Allow 1 duck for each 2 persons.
[*Serves 2 to 4*]

Sea Duck

SEA DUCK STEW

The black ducks known as scoters or coots and the old
squaws and golden-eyes can be used in stew. Skin out
the breasts and remove. Discard everything else. Soak
the breasts overnight, or at least 6 hours before cooking,
in a solution of 1 tablespoon salt to 1 quart water and
add 2 tablespoons vinegar. The object is to remove the
fishy flavor and odor. After discarding the salt solution
you are ready to cook.

2 pair coot breasts
   (four pieces)
Flour
Salt and pepper
¼ cup butter
1 quart water
3 tablespoons vinegar
2 teaspoons salt

2 tablespoons parsley,
   chopped
1 1-pound can tomatoes
4 carrots cut into 1-inch
   pieces
1 medium onion, sliced

After removing breasts from soaking solution, dry on
paper toweling. Dust breasts in flour to which salt and
pepper have been added. Melt butter in skillet and
brown coot breasts. Into a large, deep pot add
remaining ingredients and bring to a hard boil. Add
browned breasts to this, reduce heat, and simmer slowly
in covered pot for about 2 hours or until meat is tender.
[*Serves 3 to 4*]

Wild Duck Dinner Menu

WILD DUCK

SWEET POTATO CASSEROLE

STRING BEANS WITH MUSHROOMS

PINEAPPLE GRAPEFRUIT MOLD

CORN MUFFINS

MACAROON PIE

COFFEE

WINE, A GOOD CLARET

Recipes for all accompaniments follow in the next section.

Wild Goose

The wild goose of any species is a deceptive bird. It appears much larger than it actually is. An inch or more of feathers and down creates an illusion of gigantic size. And when geese have newly arrived after a long flight, there's not as much meat on the breasts as you might expect. In general a 6-pound dressed goose will serve 4-6 people.

There's more down to a goose than you'll ever want to cope with in your home. Professional plucking is highly recommended. Maybe your local cold storage plant will do this for you in exchange for a small fee.

Most people who cook wild geese regularly do not suggest stuffing this bird. The stuffing will have a tendency to become bitter. Usually an apple or celery is placed inside the cavity to absorb the bird's strong flavor. Otherwise, cooking a wild goose is much more pleasant than the same chore with a domestic bird. This is because the wild goose has far less fat to mess up your oven.

ROASTED YOUNG GOOSE

A small young goose, or a small goose species, such as the brant found on both coasts, may be cooked easily. Place your goose on a rack in a shallow pan lined with aluminum foil. Roast it in a 400-425°F. oven for 35-45 minutes. Season well with salt and pepper. Serve when tender.

CANADIAN GOOSE IN BAG

Personally, I like a clean kitchen. This recipe makes it easy to maintain mine. Maybe that's why I find it the best.

1 tablespoon flour	2 tablespoons whole celery
1 cup dry, red wine	seed
1 goose (about 6 pounds	2 teaspoons whole celery
dressed)	seed
Salt	

Preheat oven to 350°F. Shake 1 tablespoon flour within a large size (14 x 20-inch) oven cooking bag and place in a 2-inch deep roasting pan. Pour wine into bag and stir with flour until well mixed. Remove excess fat from inside the goose, rinse and pat dry. Season cavity and outside with salt. Place 2 tablespoons whole celery seed inside the body cavity and sprinkle 2 teaspoons whole celery seed on the outside of the goose.

Place goose within the bag and close bag with twist-tie. Make 6 ½-inch slits in top of bag. Cook for 2 hours (adjust cooking time for larger or smaller bird). Remove goose to serving platter and pour gravy from bag into a small saucepan. Skim off grease, bring gravy to a boil and serve with the goose.

DIANA'S ROASTED GOOSE

Maryland's Eastern Shore is a fabulous place for goose
shooting and good living. This recipe was developed by
Mrs. Diana Mautz, a dentist's wife and sailing
enthusiast, of St. Michaels, Maryland. It is terrific.
However, let me warn you to roast a goose in this
manner only if you have a self-cleaning oven.

Preheat your oven to 500°F. Remove any excess fat
from inside goose, rinse and pat dry. Put a generous
amount of Kosher salt, a coarse grain salt very flavorful
in game cooking, within the body cavity and all over
the outside of the goose. Place several tablespoons of
whole celery seed inside the body cavity and sprinkle a
generous amount of this celery seed on the surface of
the goose. Place goose upon a rack within a shallow pan
lined with aluminum foil, or on a roasting pan arranged
so fat can drip through. Roast uncovered for 1 hour.
Then turn oven off and allow goose to remain in oven
for another hour WITHOUT OPENING DOOR! The
result is great gastronomically but a mess to clean up
after.

Diana's Roasted Goose is especially good with baked acorn squash and Brussels sprouts.

GOOSE PATÉ

All goose leftovers are delicious when served cold the following day. If you'd like to do something really special with them, try this recipe from Kathy McCormick.

2 cups cooked goose, cubed	Mayonnaise
¾ cup celery, chopped	Softened butter
½ cup onion	Salt and pepper to taste
¼ cup vermouth	

Run the first four ingredients through your blender. Add butter and mayonnaise until you reach an easy-to-spread consistency. (This is a matter of personal preference as some people like a spread to be stiff and others prefer it very soft.) Add salt and pepper to taste and serve on toast points.

Wild Goose Dinner Menu

WILD GOOSE

HOMINY GRITS

BAKED ACORN SQUASH

BEET HORSERADISH RING

BEER MUFFINS

BAKED APPLES

PUMPKIN BREAD

COFFEE

WINE, A SPARKLING BURGUNDY

Recipes for all accompaniments follow.

ACCOMPANIMENTS

"It's not what you do, it's the way that you do it" was the refrain of a popular song when I was very young. The way you serve game, and the starches, vegetables and desserts you serve with it, are important to the enjoyment of the game. A good wine can add to the pleasure of any meal. Maybe I'm not much of a connoisseur, but the California and New York State varieties suit me just fine. After all, why not an American wine with American game?

The following all have been well-tested and run the gauntlet of family and friends on many occasions. As with everything in this book, you will find them easy to prepare and very good eating. Enjoy them!

Starches

B & O SPOON BREAD

Back in the wonderful days when I was a little girl in a small, West Virginia town, one of life's greatest thrills was traveling on the railroad. Of course, there was only one railroad that mattered, at least to me. It was the Baltimore & Ohio with its beautifully decorated dining cars and their special blue and white china decorated with pictures of Harper's Ferry and other famous scenes along the right-of-way.

Time has not dealt gently with the railroads. The huge smokepuffing, steam locomotives, the parlor cars, even the wonderful dining cars with their smiling, white-jacketed waiters, are gone except from our memories. But the spoon bread they served on the B&O will last as long as Americans appreciate good cooking.

This is the original recipe. It was given to me by my mother who in turn obtained it from the chief chef of the entire B&O Railroad. Mother appreciates good spoon bread and is herself an excellent cook. Would you believe she studied under Fannie Farmer? Yes, Fannie Farmer was a real person who taught cooking and home economics at Columbia University many years ago. As a young student, Mother was in Fannie Farmer's final class.

2 cups milk
1 cup white corn meal
2 tablespoons melted
   butter

3 egg yolks, thoroughly
   beaten
1 teaspoon baking powder
½ teaspoon salt
3 egg whites, stiffly
   beaten

Preheat oven to 350°F. Into 2 cups boiling milk, stir 1 cup corn meal. Place over slow, direct heat and stir gently until milk and corn meal are blended and thick. Add melted butter and let mixture cool. Do *not* chill. Add beaten egg yolks, baking powder and salt. When ready to bake, fold in stiffly beaten egg whites. Pour into a well-greased 1 ½ quart Pyrex baking dish and bake for 45 minutes.

[*Serves 4*]

VEGETABLE YAM CASSEROLE

You will find this a superb dish that can be easily prepared on the morning of a dinner party and then heated up for evening serving.

6 medium yams, cooked or canned

1 small head cauliflower, cooked and broken into flowerets

2 cups cooked green peas, drained

3 tablespoons parsley, chopped

½ cup cheddar cheese, grated

3 tablespoons butter or margarine, melted

Preheat oven to 325°F. Arrange yams, cauliflowerets and peas in greased 1½ quart casserole. Sprinkle with parsley and cheese before adding butter and bake for 25 to 30 minutes. If you prepare this ahead of time, store completed casserole in refrigerator. Do not bake. Before serving, bring dish to room temperature and then bake according to instructions.

[*Serves 6*]

BREAD DUMPLINGS

This is a Wisconsin recipe that Rose Spanel was kind enough to give me. She in turn learned it from her mother-in-law. It's good and easy to make.

½ loaf bread
1 egg
2 tablespoons shortening
1-1 ¼ cups of milk

½ teaspoon salt
¼ - ½ cup flour
Salted water

Crumble bread and set out about 1 hour until dry. Add egg and shortening to bread. Pour enough milk (1-1 ¼ cups) into bread to form a sticky mixture. Add salt and enough flour (not over ½ cup) to form a soft ball. Too much flour will create a pasty taste. Drop dumplings into a deep pan of boiling salted water and boil about 15 minutes. When done, take dumplings from water and let them dry out for a few minutes before serving with butter.

[*Serves 4 to 6*]

TANGERINE SWEET POTATO CASSEROLE

This dish goes very well with every game recipe and is especially good in cold weather when you want something to stick to your ribs and when both sweet potatoes and tangerines are available.

2 pounds (about 6 medium) sweet potatoes, cooked and peeled
¼ cup melted butter
6 tablespoons firmly packed brown sugar
3 tablespoons dark rum
½ teaspoon salt

4 tangerines
¼ cup pecans, chopped

Preheat oven to 375°F. Place small size (10 x 16-inch) oven cooking bag in 2-inch deep roasting pan. Mash sweet potatoes, whip in butter, brown sugar, rum, and salt. Peel tangerines, removing white membrane. Cut tangerine sections into halves and remove seeds. Fold tangerine pieces and chopped pecans into sweet potato mixture. Pour into bag. Close bag with twist tie and make 6 ½-inch slits in top. Bake for 30 minutes. [*Serves 6*]

OVEN BAKED ORANGE RICE

Bill Satterfield sent me this recipe from Birmingham, Alabama, where he now lives and works. When you try it, you'll agree with me that this is one man who really can cook.

¾ cup regular long
  grain rice
⅔ cup celery, chopped
2 tablespoons onion,
  chopped
2 tablespoons melted
  butter
1 tablespoon orange peel,
  grated
1 teaspoon salt

¾ cup orange juice
1 ¼ cups water

Preheat oven to 350°F. Mix rice, celery, onion, butter, orange peel and salt together and pour into a buttered 1-quart casserole. Heat orange juice and water together in a saucepan to boiling. Add orange juice mixture to casserole and stir. Cover and bake about 45 minutes or until rice is fluffy and tender.
[*Serves 4*]

Vegetables

SWEET AND SOUR RED CABBAGE

This goes well with every type of game. It was
developed in Germany where both hunting and eating
game are considered fine arts. If you make this red
cabbage from the raw ingredients, it means a
considerable amount of work. Mrs. Christine Wagner of
Churchville, Pennsylvania, explained to me that her
recipe is even better and much easier than starting from
scratch. Having tried it, I completely agree.

2 16-ounce jars sweet and   1 1-pound can of
   sour red cabbage   applesauce

Always use two parts red cabbage to one part of
applesauce and you can make as much or as little as you
need. Just combine the cabbage with the applesauce
and place in a saucepan. Cover with a loose lid and
cook very slowly on top of your stove until most of the
liquid has evaporated. This will take 1 to 1½ hours.
[*Serves 6*]

BAKED ACORN SQUASH

People who aren't crazy about some forms of squash
often enjoy this. After experimenting with several
methods, I found it was the easiest and best way to cook
it successfully.

3 acorn squash   2 tablespoons brown sugar
6 tablespoons butter   Salt and pepper

Preheat oven to 350°F. Place family size, (14 x 20-inch) oven cooking bag in 2-inch deep roasting pan. Cut each squash in half and spoon out seeds. Arrange squash halves in bag with skin down and hollow side up. Place one tablespoon butter and 1 teaspoon brown sugar in each cavity and season with salt and pepper. Close bag with twist-tie and make 6 ½-inch slits in top of bag. Cook for 45 minutes or until tested done.
[*Serves 6*]

CARROT SOUFFLÉ

This is an unusual way to prepare carrots. The consistency, color and flavor of this dish almost makes you think you used pumpkin.

2 pounds carrots raw or frozen
½ stick butter (or ¼ cup melted butter)
½ cup sugar
1 egg

¼ cup evaporated milk
⅓ cup flour
1 ½ teaspoon cinnamon
1 ½ teaspoon baking powder

Preheat oven to 350°F. Peel and slice raw carrots into thin rings. Boil and mash. Add butter, sugar and beat in egg. Add remaining ingredients and stir well. Then bake in a greased 1-quart baking dish for about 50 minutes or until a knife comes out clean.
[*Serves 6*]

BRUSSELS SPROUTS ORIENTAL

Ordinarily, Brussels sprouts are not the world's most exciting vegetable. Here's a way to make them become outstanding.

2 pounds Brussels sprouts, washed and trimmed
Salted water
1 teaspoon soy sauce
½ teaspoon salt
1 tablespoon butter or margarine
1 5-ounce can water chestnuts, drained and sliced

Simmer Brussels sprouts, covered, in a small amount of salted water for about 8 to 10 minutes until tender. Drain, add remaining ingredients and heat. Serve hot.
[*Serves 6*]

STRING BEANS WITH MUSHROOMS

Here's a way of jazzing up string beans that works wonders.

2 or 3 packages frozen string beans (or 1 ½ pounds fresh string beans)
1 4-ounce can sliced mushrooms
2 tablespoons butter or margarine
Salt and pepper

Cook beans, drain off water, add mushrooms without liquid and top off with butter or margarine. Salt and pepper to taste.
[*Serves 6*]

ARTICHOKE HEARTS AND SPINACH SOUFFLÉ

Of course this sounds like an unusual combination. Try it and you'll be amazed how quickly it vanishes.

2 cans whole artichoke hearts (12-14 hearts per can)

1 package frozen spinach soufflé

Preheat oven to 350°F. Let spinach souffle thaw and snip off the pointed ends of the artichoke hearts. Then place the artichoke hearts upright not touching one another, in a greased flat pan. Spoon the spinach soufflé onto the top of each heart. Then place in oven for 25-30 minutes or until artichoke hearts are heated through.
[*Serves 6*]

ORANGE GLAZED CARROTS

One of my personal favorites, carrots are a vegetable that team well with game.

⅓ cup sugar
1 tablespoon flour
¾ teaspoon salt
2 teaspoons grated orange peel
¾ cup orange juice

2 tablespoons butter or margarine
1 pound carrots (already cooked) or
1 20-ounce package frozen carrots

Mix sugar, flour, salt and orange peel. Add orange juice and cook until thickened. Add butter and pour glaze over cooked carrots.
[*Serves 6*]

Salads

SPINACH SALAD

Remember Popeye the Sailor Man? If he'd eaten his
spinach this way, he might have enjoyed it still more.

1 10-ounce package fresh
  spinach
½ teaspoon salt
½ clove garlic

½ teaspoon dry mustard
2 drops Tabasco sauce
3 tablespoons lemon juice
7 tablespoons salad oil
Fresh ground pepper

Soak and wash each spinach leaf. Dry on towel.
Sprinkle salt over wooden salad bowl and rub with
garlic. Discard garlic. Add other ingredients to bowl for
dressing. Tear spinach into small pieces and place over
dressing. Mix thoroughly just before serving. If you
wish, add croutons.
[*Serves 6 to 8*]

WALDORF SALAD

This apple salad is a favorite of mine, especially during
fall and winter when apples are in season.

2 cups apples, diced
Dash of salt
1 cup celery, chopped
½ cup broken walnuts

½ cup raisins (optional)
¼ cup mayonnaise
¼ cup light cream

Combine first five ingredients. Then add mayonnaise
and cream. Stir gently. Chill in refrigerator and serve in
lettuce-lined salad bowl.
[*Serves 6*]

114

AVOCADO WITH FRENCH DRESSING

Some call this a salad, others an appetizer. No matter
what you call it, serve and enjoy it. Preparation is easy.
Cut avocados in half and remove the large central pit.
Fill hollows with French dressing and serve.
[*One avocado serves 2 persons*]

Here's my mother's special recipe for French dressing.

2 tablespoons sugar
1 dash each of salt,
    pepper, paprika, and
    Cayenne pepper
3 tablespoons catsup

½ cup salad oil
½ cup vinegar
1 tablespoon water

Place all ingredients into a pint jar following suggested
order. Shake well and store in refrigerator.
[*Makes 1½ cups*]

WHOLE CRANBERRY SAUCE

Do you realize there are places where you can go fishing and see wild cranberries growing? This recipe is sure-fire with game.

2 cups sugar
1 cup water

1 pound (4 cups) fresh
  cranberries
2 teaspoons grated orange
  rind (optional)

Combine sugar and water in saucepan and stir to dissolve sugar. Bring to a boil and boil for 5 minutes. Add cranberries and orange rind and cook until skins pop. This takes about 5 minutes longer. Remove from heat and serve either warm or chilled.
[*Serves 6 to 8*]

KATHY'S PINEAPPLE BAKE

A hot salad? Why not? My children sulk when I serve this to company and too little remains for them. It's an Eastern Shore recipe that lends a touch of glamour to any game dish.

3 eggs beaten
1 stick butter (¼ pound)
  melted
4 pieces regular white
  bread, crumbled

1 20-ounce can crushed
  pineapple, undrained
½ cup sugar

Preheat oven to 425°F. Beat 3 eggs and add remaining ingredients. Mix well and pour into a 2-quart baking dish or casserole. Then bake for 25 minutes. Serve hot.
[*Serves 4 to 6*]

PEACH CHUTNEY

During peach season it's often so hot you wish fall and
hunting would hurry up and arrive. Instead of merely
wishing, you can prepare for future game meals by
making this easy recipe for peach chutney. It goes well
with venison, small game, gamebirds and waterfowl. I
discovered this recipe when a jar was given my by a
friendly neighbor, Mrs. Josephine Bloomer, a superb
cook.

3 ½ cups sugar
2 cups white vinegar

1 quart ripe peaches,
    peeled and chopped
    (6 medium size
    peaches)
1 ½ cups raisins
1 clove garlic, minced
1 piece ginger root,
    peeled, chopped or
    3 pieces preserved or
    candied ginger,
    chopped

In a pot heat sugar and vinegar to boiling. Add
remaining ingredients and bring again to a boil. Cook
slowly, uncovered, for 2 hours or until thick, stirring
occasionally. Ladle into 4 hot, sterilized, ½-pint jars
and seal.
[*Makes 2 pints*]

PINEAPPLE GRAPEFRUIT MOLD

This salad is right with game because it is not too sweet.

2 8-ounce cans crushed
    pineapple (drain and
    hold juice)
1 1-pound can grapefruit
    sections (drain and
    hold juice)

2 packages lemon Jello
2 8-ounce containers
    pineapple yogurt

Drain fruit well and reserve liquid. Add water to juice
if necessary to make 2 full cups. Bring liquid to boiling
and add Jello. Cool until syrupy; add yogurt. Fold in
fruit and pour into large mold. Chill and serve cold
with sour cream.
[*Serves 8 to 10*]

BEET HORSERADISH RING

They say there's no accounting for tastes. Both my
husband and I love the taste of this tangy salad.

1 cup julienne beets
    (drain and reserve
    juice)
1 3-ounce package lemon
    Jello
½ cup boiling water

1 cup beet juice (from
    beets)
3 tablespoons vinegar
4 tablespoons horseradish

Drain beets and reserve 1 cup of beet juice. Dissolve
lemon Jello in ½ cup boiling water. Add vinegar and
beet juice. When slightly thickened, add beets and
horseradish. Pour into small mold and chill.
[*Serves 4 to 6*]

Hot Breads

DROP BISCUITS

You'll like this recipe because you don't have to roll or knead the dough. The lard makes these biscuits light.

2 cups biscuit mix   ½ cup cold water
2 tablespoons lard

Preheat oven to 450°F. and grease baking sheet. Place biscuit mix in a bowl and cut in lard with pastry blender. Add water and mix ingredients with fork until you arrive at a soft dough. Spoon this dough onto baking sheet allowing 1 spoonful for each biscuit. Bake 8 to 10 minutes until ready.
[*Makes 10 to 12 nice biscuits*]

CORN MUFFINS

There's something about piping hot corn muffins . . .

1 ¼ cups corn meal   ½ teaspoon salt
¾ cup sifted all-purpose   1 egg
   flour   1 cup milk
¼ cup sugar   ¼ cup vegetable oil
1 tablespoon baking
   powder

Preheat oven to 425°F. Sift together corn meal, flour, sugar, baking powder and salt in a bowl. Add egg, milk and vegetable oil. Beat with rotary beater until smooth. This will take about 1 minute. Fill greased muffin cups ⅔ full. Bake 15 to 20 minutes.
[*Makes 12 medium-size muffins*]

BEER MUFFINS

The South is the home of good hot breads, and this recipe is traditional in this region.

6 ounces (½ can or bottle) warm beer
1 ½ tablespoons sugar

1 ½ cups biscuit mix

Preheat oven to 425°F. Pour beer into medium bowl. Add sugar and beat until sugar dissolves. Mixture will be foamy. Now add biscuit mix and stir until well moistened. Do *not* overstir. Grease muffin tins and allow a heaping tablespoon of batter for each muffin. Let rise for 20 minutes and then bake for 15 minutes or until lightly browned.

[*Makes 9 to 10 muffins*]

Desserts

MINCEMEAT CAKE

Wonderful for a festive evening, this cake may be served with hard sauce as an extra treat.

1 cup brown sugar
½ cup margarine or soft shortening
2 cups all purpose flour
1 16-ounce jar mincemeat
1 cup dates, chopped
1 cup nuts, chopped

1 tablespoon soda
1 tablespoon hot water
1 teaspoon vanilla extract
2 egg yolks
2 egg whites, stiffly beaten

Preheat oven to 300°F. Cream sugar and shortening until light and fluffy. Mix ½ cup flour with mincemeat, dates and nuts. Dissolve soda in hot water. Combine all ingredients except egg whites and blend well. Fold in stiffly beaten egg whites and spoon into a greased, paper-lined, 9 x 5 x 3-inch loaf pan. Bake 1½ to 2 hours.

[*Makes 16 slices*]

HARD SAUCE

⅓ cup butter, room temperature

1 tablespoon bourbon or brandy

1-1½ cups confectioners sugar

Pinch of salt

Work the butter with a spoon until light and creamy. Add bourbon and mix with butter. Add sugar gradually until light and fluffy. Chill until time to serve.

RAW APPLE CAKE

This is a very old recipe, and you must NOT use an electric mixer. The result is a cake which is moist and keeps exceptionally well. It's extra delicious served with a scoop of vanilla ice cream.

1 ½ cups vegetable oil
3 eggs, slightly beaten
1 teaspoon vanilla
1 teaspoon salt
1 teaspoon cinnamon
2 cups sugar

3 cups flour
1 teaspoon baking soda
3 cups raw peeled apples, chopped
1 cup nuts, chopped (optional)

Grease a 10-inch tube pan thoroughly. Combine all ingredients except apples and nuts and stir until well blended and moist. Then add apples and nuts and bake for 1 hour at 375°F. Sprinkle confectioners sugar on top if you like.
[*Makes 16 to 20 servings*]

STUFFED BAKED APPLES

One reason I'm including this recipe is it's the fastest, neatest way of baking apples I've ever tried.

6 large baking apples
¼ cup firmly packed brown sugar
3 tablespoons soft butter
3 tablespoons slivered almonds (optional)
2 tablespoons apricot preserves

¼ teaspoon salt
¾ cup orange juice
½ cup sugar
2 teaspoons quick-cooking tapioca

Preheat oven to 350° F. Place family size (14 x 20-inch) oven cooking bag in 2-inch deep roasting pan. Core apples, leaving a small plug in bottom end. Pare skin from upper half of each apple. Combine brown sugar, butter, almonds, apricot preserves and salt. Fill apples with this mixture. Place apples in oven bag. Combine orange juice, sugar and tapioca and pour mixture over apples. Close bag with twist-tie and make 6 ½-inch slits on top. Bake 30 minutes or until tested tender. To serve cut open top of bag and lift apples out. Spoon juice over apples.

[*Serves 6*]

MACAROON PIE

This pie is different — crunchy, chewy, crustless.

16 saltines, finely rolled
16 pitted dates, finely
  chopped
½ cup pecans, chopped
1 cup sugar

¼ teaspoon baking
  powder
3 egg whites
Whipped cream or vanilla
  ice cream

Preheat oven to 350° F. Blend saltines, dates, pecans and sugar. Add baking powder to egg whites and beat until stiff but not dry. Fold egg whites into saltine mixture and spread in well-buttered, 9-inch pie plate. Bake 30 minutes. Cool, serve topped with whipped cream or ice cream.

[*Serves 6 to 8*]

NO-ROLL PASTRY SHELL

This isn't something you buy at the store. It's a quick recipe that leaves no mess and I use it with pumpkin pie and pineapple meringue pie. The following is for a single 8-inch or 9-inch crust.

1 ½ cups sifted all purpose flour
1 ½ teaspoons sugar
1 teaspoon salt

½ cup vegetable oil
2 tablespoons cold milk

Place dry ingredients in pie pan. Combine oil and milk in measuring cup. Whip with fork and pour over flour mixture all at once. Mix with fork until flour is completely dampened. Press the resulting dough evenly and firmly with your fingers to line first the bottom of your pan, and then the sides and partly cover the rim. Make sure the dough is pressed to a uniform thickness all around. Fill as desired and bake in hot oven at 400° F. for 15 minutes and then reduce heat to 350° F. until filling is done. If you want to make a baked shell, prick the entire surface and bake in hot 425° F. oven for 12 to 15 minutes. Remove, cool and fill as desired.

PINEAPPLE MERINGUE PIE

Most of us associate Hawaii with pineapple but not with hunting. There is hunting for deer, pheasant, wild boar and also wild turkey on the islands of Lanai, Molokai, Kauai and Hawaii itself, along with some unusual hunting for wild goat and sheep, the descendants of those set ashore by sailors centuries ago.

6 tablespoons cornstarch	4 eggs, separated
1 cup sugar, divided	2 tablespoons lemon juice
½ teaspoon salt	1 baked 10-inch No-Roll
2 20-ounce cans crushed	pastry shell (see
pineapple, undrained	preceding recipe)

Preheat oven to 425°F. Combine cornstarch, ½ cup of sugar, salt and undrained pineapple in a saucepan. Cook over low heat stirring constantly until mixture is thickened and clear. Beat egg yolks and add a little of hot mixture to them. Return yolks to saucepan and add lemon juice before cooking 1 minute. Then cool and place in baked No-Roll pie shell. Beat egg whites until stiff but not dry. Slowly add remaining ½ cup of sugar and swirl over top of pie. Bake entire pie for 4 minutes. [*Serves 8 to 10*]

PUMPKIN PIE

Of course you can start with raw pumpkin. But this is a good, time-saving recipe.

1 ½ cups canned pumpkin
¾ cup brown sugar
2 eggs, beaten
1 ½ cups milk
½ teaspoon vanilla

½ teaspoon salt
1 tablespoon pumpkin pie spice
1 unbaked 9-inch No-Roll pastry shell (see preceding recipe)

Preheat oven to 400°F. Mix well in order above. Pour into unbaked, 9-inch No-Roll pastry shell. Bake 15 minutes in hot oven until crust is set. Then reduce to 350°F. and bake until filling is firm about 30 minutes. This recipe makes one pie which may be topped with whipped cream if desired.
[*Serves 8*]

PUMPKIN RAISIN NUT BREAD

Theresa Wallace from Alabama gave me this recipe which doesn't require a mixer. Even better, it makes two loaves at once and you can put one in your freezer to use later.

1 cup vegetable oil
4 eggs
⅔ cup water
2 cups mashed pumpkin
3 ⅓ cups flour
1 ½ teaspoons salt

1 teaspoon nutmeg
2 teaspoons soda
1 teaspoon cinnamon
3 cups sugar
½ cup raisins
½ cup nuts, chopped

Preheat oven to 350° F. Grease and flour two
8½ x 4½ x 3-inch loaf pans. Combine oil, eggs, water
and pumpkin. Sift dry ingredients and make a hollow
in the center in which you pour the liquid pumpkin
mixture all at once. Stir until flour is moist. Mix in
raisins and nuts. Bake 1 hour.
[*Each cake yields 16 slices*]

CHILLED ORANGE SLICES IN RED WINE

A fruit dessert often seems to go well with a heavy game
dinner and oranges are at their best during the winter
when most game is served. By using an oven bag with
this recipe you have dependable wonderful results and
no cleaning up.

6 large navel oranges	2 cloves
¾ cup sugar	1 stick cinnamon
1 cup water	2 slices tangerine
1 cup dry, red wine	2 slices lemon

Preheat oven to 400°F. Place family size (14 x 20-inch)
oven cooking bag in 2-inch deep roasting pan. Remove
any seeds from oranges and place slices within bag.
Dissolve sugar in water and add wine. Tie cloves,
cinnamon, tangerine and lemon in cheesecloth. Pour
wine mixture over orange slices, and place spice-filled
bag in middle of oven bag. Close oven bag with
twist-tie and make 6 ½-inch slits in top. Cook for 25
minutes. Let mixture cool to room temperature.
Refrigerate until very cold. Remove spice bag. Serve this
dessert cold.
[*Serves 6*]

CHEESE CAKE WITH GRAHAM CRACKER CRUST

My family tells me this is better than any cheese cake you can buy at a store or restaurant. After having served it for years, I've yet to find anyone who disagrees.

Crust:

Begin by making the graham cracker crust in a 9-inch spring form. Do it by mixing 1¼ cups of graham cracker crumbs with ¼ cup confectioners powdered sugar, and ¼ cup melted butter or margarine. Pour crumb mixture into a 9-inch spring form and press mixture firmly against bottom and sides of pan.

Filling:

3 8-ounce packages cream cheese	½ teaspoon vanilla
	Juice of ½ lemon
¾ cup sugar	1 pint sour cream
4 eggs	2 tablespoons sugar

Preheat oven to 325° F. Cream the cheese and sugar; add eggs one at a time. Stir in vanilla and lemon juice. Pour mixture into the crumb-lined spring form and bake for 40 minutes. Mix 1 pint sour cream with 2 tablespoons sugar. Spread this mixture on top of the hot cheese cake and return to oven for 10 minutes. Let cake cool and refrigerate. Remove from spring form before serving.
[*Serves 10 to 12*]

MICROWAVE OVEN RECIPES

Not everyone owns a microwave oven. If you do, you'll find it excellent for cooking small quantities of game birds and animals. Because these ovens cook so rapidly, they seal in the juices and help keep game moist and succulent.

With the early microwave ovens, browning was a problem. Today, the ovens often have special browning elements. Also, you can use a special browning skillet which is preheated in your oven and allows you to sear your meat or bird, thereby browning it.

Still another browning method involves the use of a mixture of honey and Kitchen Bouquet that is brushed over your game before cooking it.

What about cooking times? These are going to vary with each make and model of oven. Those given here must be looked upon as approximations only. Size and thickness of steaks and chops are other factors. Unlike conventional cooking, microwave cooking involves an amount of time directly proportionate to the quantity of food being cooked. It will take you twice as long to cook two quail as it does to cook one.

With the above in mind, I recommend the following recipes. They've come in handy on occasions when I've demonstrated game cookery before an audience and needed the ultra-short cooking time that microwave ovens provide.

MICROWAVE VENISON STEAK

Preheat browning skillet for 5 minutes in the microwave oven. Place 2 tablespoons butter in the hot skillet and immediately add one small, individual-size, ½-inch thick venison steak. Cook for 1½ minutes. Remove skillet from oven, turn steak and cook 1½ minutes on opposite side. Remove steak from oven and salt and pepper to taste. The steak should be faintly pink when cut.

You'll find this same method is useful in cooking venison chops. Always remember your cooking time relates directly to the number of chops or steaks, their size and thickness.

MICROWAVE DOVE

4 doves, split down back	Salt
Flour	2 tablespoons Madeira
4 tablespoons butter	wine

Dust doves lightly in flour. Preheat browning skillet for 5 minutes in microwave oven. Place 4 tablespoons of butter in hot skillet and immediately place doves in skillet skin side down. Cook 2½ minutes, remove, turn doves over and cook 2½ minutes again. Remove doves from skillet and sprinkle with salt. Add 2 tablespoons of Madeira wine to drippings in skillet, stir and serve over doves.

[*Allow 3 per person*]

MICROWAVE QUAIL

For two people who have just come in from the out-of-doors, the microwave oven offers a quick hot snack in far less than usual time.

1 tablespoon flour
1 2-ounce can sliced
   mushrooms
2 quail, split down back
Salt and pepper
2 tablespoons melted
   butter
1 ½ teaspoons Kitchen
   Bouquet
½ teaspoon honey
3 tablespoons Madeira
   wine

Shake 1 tablespoon flour in small size (10 x 16-inch) Brown-In-Bag. Place bag in 1 ½-quart Pyrex dish. Add mushrooms with liquid. Season quail with salt and pepper. Combine butter, Kitchen Bouquet and honey and brush this mixture over entire surface of both quail. Place quail on top of the mushrooms and add wine. Close bag with a piece of string. You must use string instead of the metal twist-tie which comes with the bag. Otherwise, the strip of metal will interfere with the cooking process. Make 6 ½-inch slits in top of bag. Cook in microwave range for 5 minutes. Use gravy in oven bag for spooning over quail when served.
[*Allow 2 quail per person*]

INDEX

134

Photo Credits

For the use of their photographs the author thanks the following:

Page 17 — Reynolds Metals Company
Page 63 — Francis N. Satterlee, Virginia Game
            Commission
Page 67 — National Rifle Association
Page 101 — Reynolds Metals Company

When Your Local Bookstore Cannot Supply You
USE THIS FORM TO ORDER EPM BOOKS

EPM Publications - P.O. Box 442 - McLean, Va. 22101

Please send me the following EPM books

_____ copies of EASY GAME COOKING by
Joan Cone. 124 home-tested, money-
saving recipes and menus for game
birds and animals. $1.75 per copy $_____

_____ copies of INDIAN JEWELRY by
Frankie Welch. Expert advice on
buying, wearing and collecting from a
part-Cherokee fashion designer.
                            $6.95 hardcover $_____

_____ copies of RIDING THE GHOST
TOWN TRAIL by A. Frank Krause, Jr.
Compact, detailed information on
where to find ghost towns, what was
once there, and what remains. 24 black
and white photos. $2.95 per copy $_____

                            TOTAL $_____

Shipping and handling. Add 25c for 1, 2, or
3 books, 8c for every 3 additional books. $_____
(Virginia residents *please* add 4% sales tax.) $_____

Enclose check (or PO money order) for total of $_____

Name..
Address...
City......................State..........Zip.....